THE LIFE AND TIMES OF
BETTY BOOP

THE LIFE AND TIMES OF

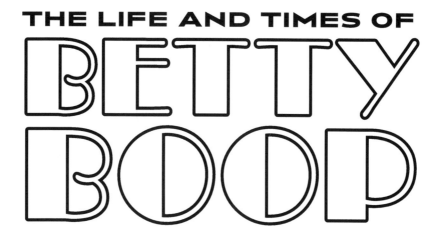

BETTY BOOP

THE 100-YEAR HISTORY OF AN ANIMATED ICON

PETER BENJAMINSON

APPLAUSE
THEATRE & CINEMA BOOKS
ESSEX, CONNECTICUT

APPLAUSE
THEATRE & CINEMA BOOKS

An imprint of Globe Pequot, the trade division of
The Rowman & Littlefield Publishing Group, Inc.
4501 Forbes Blvd., Ste. 200
Lanham, MD 20706
www.rowman.com

Distributed by NATIONAL BOOK NETWORK

Library of Congress Cataloging-in-Publication Data
Names: Benjaminson, Peter, 1945- author.
Title: The life and times of Betty Boop : the 100-year history of an animated icon /
   Peter Benjaminson.
Description: Essex, Connecticut : Applause, [2024] | Includes bibliographical
   references.
Identifiers: LCCN 2023021033 (print) | LCCN 2023021034 (ebook) |
   ISBN 9781493064281 (paperback) | ISBN 9781493064298 (ebook)
Subjects: LCSH: Boop, Betty (Fictitious character) | Cartoon characters—United
   States—History. | Animated films—United States—History and criticism. | Comic
   strip characters—United States—History. | Comic books, strips, etc.—United
   States—History and criticism. | Fleischer, Max, 1883-1972.
Classification: LCC NC1766.U52 F5832 2024 (print) | LCC NC1766.U52 (ebook) |
   DDC 741.5/6973—dc23/eng/20230801
LC record available at https://lccn.loc.gov/2023021033
LC ebook record available at https://lccn.loc.gov/2023021034

♾™ The paper used in this publication meets the minimum requirements of American National Standard for Information Sciences—Permanence of Paper for Printed Library Materials, ANSI/NISO Z39.48-1992

CONTENTS

PREFACE

I'm happy as I am and love my liberty too well to be
in a hurry to give it up for any mortal man.

—Louisa May Alcott

Although the Great Depression was well underway by 1930, when
Betty Boop first appeared on movie screens, people didn't go to movie
theaters to be reminded of their economic distress: they went to escape
it. And one way Betty's creators could swiftly whisk them back to the
happier days of the 1920s was to bring back the flappers, the much-
discussed liberated women of that decade. Like Betty, these unmarried,
pleasure-seeking young women wore short skirts, drove automobiles,
and flouted many social and sexual standards. They were often seen as
jazz-crazed single girls who smoked, danced, drank, sang, and flirted
with boys and men in speakeasys.

Recent events had inspired them. World War I and the 1918 flu
pandemic had killed at least 77 million people in countries around the
world, including 400,000 in the United States, causing many young
women to think only of today instead of tomorrow. They also concentrated less on getting married: being single wasn't such a big deal

anymore. These young women also felt independent for other reasons. In 1920, just ten years earlier, American women had finally won the right to vote, and their growing use of automobiles was making it much easier for them to travel.

Such developments caused many of them to become individuals in their own right, creating and maintaining their own careers and not being dissuaded by men, or marriage, from taking the career path they chose. In fact, they often referred to wedding rings as "handcuffs" or "manacles." They also were much less interested in staying at home whether they were married or not. Betty, a cartoon, comic strip, and movie character, was in many ways a flapper herself, much more focused on a career than she was on getting married. In fact, she never married or seemed to have had children.

There were some differences between Betty and the flappers, however. Many flappers wore bras that flattened their breasts so they could dance vigorously without their breasts bouncing. They took this measure partly to emphasize that they should be taken seriously in nonsexual contexts. (They were called "flappers" because one of their habits was to wear their boots open and flapping, rather than fastened.) Betty's animators, who were almost all male, gave Betty a prominent bustline. In any case, styles soon began changing. In its April 1932 issue, *Vogue* magazine announced that "Spring styles say CURVES!" and Betty became, essentially, a curvy flapper.

Although many Americans had disapproved of flappers during the 1920s, they remembered them and their boyish bobs; spit curls; round faces; wide, mascaraed eyes; and squeaky voices with great fondness in the 1930s. Partly as a result, Betty climbed to, and maintained, her peak of popularity from the time she was created in 1930 until the

Movie Production Code, also known as the Hays Code, was imposed on animated cartoons and movies in 1934. She continued as a cartoon star until 1939, however, appearing in ninety animated features during the 1930s. She also starred in her own daily and Sunday comic strips from 1934 until 1937 and continues to appear today in numerous animated television specials, videos, comic books, and graphic novels. She became a Lancôme video star in 2012, a Zac Posen heroine in 2017, and the star of Betty Boop Apps in 2020. Several movies and musicals about her are in the planning stages. Betty was also the Most Popular Balloon at the Macy's Thanksgiving Day parade for several years, as well as the model for numerous musical groups and a mascot for sports teams in several countries.

Her underlying appeal to her numerous female fans became starkly evident in a crucial scene in *The Romance of Betty Boop*, an animated TV show that was released in 1985 but set in the 1930s. In the show, it becomes clear that Freddy, Betty's most serious recent boyfriend, has been courting her for years. She's recently broken up with another man and is standing on her apartment balcony when she sees Freddy walking down the street. It suddenly dawns on her that he has always been the right man for her. Her script writers had her yell down to him, "You were Mr. Right all along!" and admit that she'd been wrong to reject him.

Overjoyed, Freddy runs up the stairs and joins Betty on the balcony. Then, while the two of them hug and stare into each other's eyes, they sing "I Only Have Ice for You" (almost identical to the hit 1934 song "I Only Have Eyes for You"; Freddy's job, in those days before electric refrigerators, is to deliver large chunks of ice to homeowners and apartment dwellers), and kiss.

"You're so super!" Betty says.

Just then, her phone rings: a movie studio is asking her to fly to Hollywood for a screen test. "It's the chance of a lifetime!" she tells Freddy. "What should I do?"

He looks dismayed. Hadn't they just answered that question? To Betty, the answer is obvious: she'll forget about Freddy, fly west, and become a star.

For nearly a century, that decision has made Betty a heroine to, and an example for, millions of women. Life isn't all about men, but about *you*, Betty says, and during the course of her long and possibly endless life, at the instigation of her creators, producers, directors, and animators, she's kept on demonstrating just that.

Betty's conduct on-screen and in comic strips was heavily influenced by numerous real-world events besides changing gender norms. Among those developments was a severe rise in joblessness and homelessness during the Great Depression; the resulting increase in racial and religious discrimination by white Americans against African Americans, Native Americans, Asian Americans, and Italian Americans; a rise in discrimination by American Protestants against Catholics and Jews; an escalating high school dropout rate and a corresponding decrease in college attendance; and the incendiary and frightening growth of fascism and Nazism. As a result, as writer G. Michael Dobbs has noted, Betty's cartoons faithfully reflected a blend of emotions that characterized the 1930s: a contradictory mishmash of hope and despair, plus a mix of domesticity and wild escapist excitement.

In addition, Betty's appearance and demeanor, along with the faces and behavior of almost every other character in her animated cartoons, were heavily influenced by the location of the Fleischer Studios—which first brought her to animated life—in New York City. Especially influential was its proximity to the oddballs of Times Square; the music and dance steps being created by the jazz enthusiasts and chorines of Harlem, and the social and sexual goings-on in the apartment building in which most of the Fleischer animators lived.

Betty's career also was changed by major developments in the movie, animation, and entertainment worlds. Screenwriters, actors, and directors struggled to attract audiences to theaters while many of the members of those audiences became jobless and poor. The writers' methods included a rising use of surrealism in movies and a startling increase in the portrayal of sex on-screen before the imposition of movie censorship. Other film industry developments were also satirized or alluded to in Betty's cartoons and comic strips. They included the terrible mistreatment of Hollywood child stars, the spectacular difficulties experienced by Hollywood denizens who dared to marry each other, and the rise of numerous Hollywood divas who tried to hold themselves above the fray.

Several technical and corporate developments aided Betty's rise to the top, including her cocreator Max Fleischer's invention of the rotoscope in 1917, which he subsequently used to great advantage in popularizing Betty. (The rotoscope made it possible for animators to trace and recreate the movements of filmed live performers for use in cartoons. With these tracings as a base for his drawing, an animator could create cartoon characters who took very lifelike actions on the screen.) Also aiding Betty was the vigorous competition between the Fleischer Studios and the Walt Disney Studios during the 1930s.

Betty's rise was at times made somewhat bumpy by the film industry's prejudice against employing female animators, and differing opinions about the sexual and social mores depicted in her stories. Nonetheless, one of the many reasons Betty's cartoons attracted viewers was because some of her cartoons, for the first time in mainstream animation, dealt directly with sex. A number of her cartoons depicted her being pursued by lecherous men grabbing or fondling her on-screen. Sometimes they went further: *The Film Daily* newspaper alleged in August 1930 that in one of Betty's cartoons released that month, "Barnacle Bill," Bill makes "violent love" to Betty. While such behavior wasn't shown, at least in currently available versions of this cartoon, it's heavily implied.

At the same time, Max and Dave Fleischer, the brothers who were Betty's major creators, made her a fully female cartoon and comic strip character and feminist long before the modern women's rights movement erupted during the 1960s. Most cartoon characters before Betty had been based on semi-humanized animals, but Betty was an adult human character aimed primarily at an adult audience. Other cartoon women who preceded Betty had essentially been males with long eyelashes and skirts. But Betty was obviously a woman. She had a decidedly female shape and a convincing feminine grace to her movements and was arguably history's first sexy cartoon star.

She's not a mouse (like Minnie, Mickey Mouse's girlfriend), or a duck (like Daisy, Donald Duck's girlfriend). Moreover, she possesses no superpowers like Supergirl, Super Woman, Wonder Woman, or other similar characters. She's also not a stereotypical female character like Daisy Mae, the young woman hopelessly in love with hillbilly L'il Abner in the comic strip of that name, or Veronica, who yearns after Archie. In fact, Betty is the only classic female comic character who isn't someone's wife, girlfriend, or regular employee. Unlike Olive Oyl, Blondie, and other cartoon women, Betty's not defined by her relationship to a male character. She's an advanced modern woman, with all that description implies: she's accustomed to independence and freedom, sexual and otherwise.

Although several male characters have fallen for Betty over the years, she has never married. She's her own woman, known for herself, and not just because she belongs to some man. Although comfortable in her sexuality and interested in men, Betty remains single to this day. She also never let anyone push her around and held numerous low-level jobs before she became a stage and movie star, thus showing women how they could live independently to the fullest. Not only did Betty try and succeed in attracting men, her on-screen and on-the-page actions landed her in the middle of ongoing debates over the harassment of women in the workplace, and at other times depicted or hinted at the attraction of straight women to gay men, male erections, and S&M.

Betty is extremely flexible in the kinds of jobs she'll accept and work hard at. She's never been stuck in any single occupation, or at any one professional level. In fact, no other female cartoon or comic character has ever held as wide a range of jobs or seemed to have nurtured ambitions as lofty as hers. She started out as a nightclub singer, moved on to the legitimate stage, then became a Hollywood diva, a housewife, a pet owner, a store owner and manager, and a candidate for president twice. Betty also was employed as a waitress, a circus employee, and a penny arcade attendant. She works hard at every job she signs up for but never loses sight of her desire to rise to the top. In one story in her newspaper comic strip, the attorneys hired by her Hollywood studio are trying to trap her into signing an inappropriate movie contract. In response, she manages to find endless humorous ways to avoid signing that document without alienating her lawyers or her studio bosses. She is canny, self-controlled, and motivated enough to know that both all-male groups were essential to her Hollywood future.

While conscious of her own rights, Betty also has fought for the rights and advancement of others. In various cartoons, she hires a needy local boy to work in the store she owns, despite her own economic difficulties; does her best to provide wholesome, youthful experiences for her younger brother; and even fights for her dog's right to court an upper-class lady dog. Betty also has refused to let social restrictions interfere with her career. As a white woman living through the 1930s and on into the 1960s, she costarred in several films with African American musicians such as Louis Armstrong, Cab Calloway, and Don Redman. (Unfortunately for Betty's reputation, however, African Americans were also mocked and derided in several of her cartoons.)

As a devoted fan of Betty's, I've enjoyed watching her over the years so much that I occasionally find myself worrying more about Betty than about myself. I've applauded her wisdom on some occasions and lamented her foolishness on others. As a male, my image of how women should act, and what they can be, has been molded by Betty's views on these subjects.

My research on Betty as a multimedia character has uncovered numerous facts about her life that many of her fans are probably unaware of, one of them being that her creators lifted many of her mannerisms, including her signature saying, "boop-boop-a-doop," from Helen Kane, a famous real-life white female entertainer who'd previously copied it from at least one real-life African American female entertainer.

I was shocked to discover a few years ago that although books for young women about how they can model their behavior on Betty continue to be published, no one has ever written a book about her history as a multimedia character and a striving woman ahead of her time. After deciding it was up to me to correct this injustice, I've written my account of Betty's "life" with information gleaned from court transcripts and interviews that involved her, plus additional information that's been revealed by and about her creators and animators on several websites and in numerous animated cartoons, comic strips, comic books, books about animation, radio broadcasts, television shows, news articles, movies, and interviews.

My goal in writing this book is to show that Betty was both a product of her times and a semi-immortal animated cartoon and comic strip character. I hope that I have been successful, and that you enjoy this book about her.

1

A STAR IS BORN TO
JEWISH PARENTS

Betty's symbolic father, Max Fleischer, was born in 1883 in the city
of Krakow, then within the Austro-Hungarian Empire and now in
Poland. He was the second of six children of Jewish parents. The family spoke German, the major language of the empire.

Max immigrated to the United States with his parents when he was
four years old. The family fell on hard times after his father lost his
job as a tailor, forcing them to move from one apartment to another
until they could find one they could afford. As a teenager, Max lived
in Brownsville, a poor Jewish neighborhood in Brooklyn. He attended
evening high school classes and later studied art and illustration at Coo-
per Union in Manhattan and the Art Students League of New York.

According to Mark Fleischer and Virginia Mahoney, two of Max's
grandchildren, Max always claimed that his career as an artist had begun
when he stood up in his crib and began using a pencil to draw on the
wallpaper. But it wasn't until the turn of the century, the year 1900, that

Photograph of Max Fleischer from the June 7, 1919, issue of *The Moving Picture World*. COURTESY INTERNET ARCHIVE.

Max took decisive career action by applying for a job in the art department of the *Brooklyn Daily Eagle*. He was allegedly so eager to work there that he offered to pay that newspaper $2 a week if it would hire him. The *Eagle*'s proprietors were so pleased by this offer, and the ambition it demonstrated, that they countered by offering him $2 a week to run errands for them. Within a year he was drawing small cartoons for the paper and by 1903, he was drawing multi-panel comic strips. In 1915, Max and his younger brother Dave decided to produce their own cartoons.

Max gave the brothers their first big boost by inventing the rotoscope. Then, in 1924, working with inventor Lee DeForest, the Fleischers began adding sound to cartoons, all of which had previously been silent. That same year, the two brothers created a bouncing ball that guided theater audiences through songs the Fleischers figured they'd like to sing along with in the "Singing Car-Tunes" they soon began producing.

In 1929, they founded Fleischer Studios. (Later on, the other three Fleischer brothers, Charles, Joseph, and Lou, also became associated with the studio. A sixth brother, Saul, died at age two and their only

Illustration from Max Fleischer's 1915 patent application for the rotoscope.

sister, Ethel, became a concert pianist.) Dave, who'd worked as a clown at Coney Island Amusement Park, was the model for the Fleischer's first famous character, Koko the Clown, who appeared in the studio's *Out of the Inkwell* cartoons. Also featured in the *Inkwell* cartoon series was a small dog named Fitz, who later became Betty's pal Bimbo.

Although the Fleischers were technically skilled virtuosos who could have produced excellent cartoons under any circumstances, their studio's location at 48th Street and Broadway in Manhattan, just north of Times Square, also helped them a great deal. In one day, Fleischer

Photograph of Dave Fleischer from the February 3, 1940, issue of *Motion Picture Herald*. COURTESY INTERNET ARCHIVE.

animators could see as many weird characters through their studio windows at 1600 Broadway, or on the subway, as Walt Disney, their major competitor, probably ever saw in his life. In fact, the Fleischers soon cast their company as the sexy, dark urban alternative to Disney, whose family-friendly operation was located in sunny Burbank, California.

Because the Fleischer animators made extensive use of the city as the backdrop for many of Betty's cartoons, those weird characters appeared in those cartoons in animated form. It was no accident that while most of Disney's characters were animals, most of Fleischer's were fully or partly human. As movie critic Jami Bernard has pointed out, while Disney animators in California were "drawing characters as sunny as their surroundings, the early Fleischer studio cartoons reflected the grit, excitement, and immigrant nature of Depression-era New York. . . . Gags about poverty, death and electric chairs fill the frames of these cartoons, as do bandy-legged creatures, night terrors, and urban joie de vivre. In a Fleischer creation, the joint is always jumping."

The Fleischers' creativity was also aided by the fact that Harlem was nearby. The Fleischers and their employees spent a lot of time there, fell in love with the jazz emanating from that neighborhood in the 1920s and 1930s, and strove to use it in their cartoons. They

Times Square at night, circa 1934. The urban landscape of Manhattan was the backdrop for many of Betty's cartoons. COURTESY LIBRARY OF CONGRESS PRINTS & PHOTOGRAPHS DIVISION, LC-USZ62-54205.

also became familiar with the African American musicians who performed in Harlem, including Louis Armstrong and Cab Calloway, both of whom would eventually appear in Fleischer cartoons, but were very unlikely to be reproduced in any of Disney's animated fantasies.

In 1930, Max, working with Fleischer Studios animator Myron "Grim" Natwick, a non-Jew, created Betty Boop, the world's most famous female cartoon and comic-strip character. Grim was rarely grim. He had been tagged with his ironic nickname because he was usually very cheerful. He obviously transferred a lot of his personality to Betty: except when she was frightened out of her wits, she was buoyant and breezy.

Betty first appeared on-screen in the cartoon "Dizzy Dishes," released on August 9, 1930, in which she played a young but fully grown chanteuse in an upscale restaurant. A judge in a court case involving Betty later in the 1930s described her as having a broad baby face, large round flirting eyes, a low-placed pouting mouth, a small nose, an

Betty's first appearance, in the 1930 cartoon "Dizzy Dishes." Her origins as a doggie partner for Bimbo are still partly in evidence here.

imperceptible chin, and a mature bosom. He summed up her appearance as a "unique combination of infancy and maturity, innocence and sophistication." That was exactly the image that many women of the 1930s wished to portray.

In a reversal of nature's laws regarding aging, however, it wouldn't be until March 11, 1932, that Betty's creators got around to portraying her as a young girl in the cartoon "Minnie the Moocher." Obviously based on a satirical view of Max and Dave Fleischer's parents, relatives, and neighbors in New York City, Betty's parents in this cartoon, both Jews, are portrayed as native speakers of German who'd immigrated from Europe in the late nineteenth century. As part of their adjustment to their new country, they soon began speaking heavily accented English mixed with German and Yiddish words.

Betty's childhood as the daughter of New York Jewish immigrants in "Minnie the Moocher" (1932).

Although Betty's dad wears a yarmulke skullcap, indicating he is an Orthodox Jew, his and his wife's clothing are very similar to what most non-Jews wore at the time. The cartoon also indicates that Betty's parents, like both Jewish and non-Jewish parents, show their love for Betty by trying to overfeed her—at the very least, they want her to eat all of her dinner rather than leave most of it on the plate. The fact that Mr. and Mrs. Boop are both overweight shows that they applied the same standards to themselves at every meal. On the evening portrayed in the cartoon, her father demands that she eat large helpings of sauerbraten, a German dish consisting of beef marinated in vinegar with peppercorns and onions, and hassenpfeffer, a spicy German stew made of marinated rabbit meat. "Why don't you eat your hassenpfeffer?" Mr. Boop, voiced by actor Billy Bletcher, thunders at Betty. The Fleischers have him yelling at her so obsessively that he keeps doing so after she's fled the table in tears. Apparently, she liked her teenage figure and was determined to keep it for the rest of her life.

This was but one example of the Fleischers using Jewish stereotypes to humorous effect. In the 1930s, with the persecution of European Jews not yet at its peak, racial and religious humor was very much in vogue. It was common to mock Jews, African Americans, Latinos, Italians, Poles, and others in literature, on-screen, and in real life. As assimilated Jews, the Fleischers and their Jewish employees felt free to tease the less-assimilated ones.

Fleischer animator Shamus Culhane, who wasn't Jewish, pointed out that many of his coworkers, almost all of them young males, had at least one parent at home who was an immigrant. As a result, every animator spoke at least one foreign language as well as English, but they hated that they had to do so because they felt it made them different from other Americans. They therefore resented their parents and others who spoke Yiddish or other foreign languages or dialects, and this attitude spilled over into the cartoons they scripted and animated. As Culhane put it, "There was a fierce need to conform, and the foreign atmosphere at home was a source of embarrassment and anxiety." The young animators mocked their parents' attempts to speak English "because they were not American, and we yearned to be just that." Since animators also often doubled as script writers for Betty's cartoons, this attitude was reflected in her films.

On one hand, the mockery of Jews in Betty's cartoons usually was closer in spirit to an in-joke rather than an insult. And much to Betty's credit, she rarely participated in the mildly anti-Semitic behavior that appeared in her films. On the other hand, many of the characterizations in her cartoons would almost certainly be considered anti-Semitic if shown today.

It began almost imperceptibly in Betty's first cartoon, "Dizzy Dishes." A man-dog character named Bimbo is working as a chef and a waiter in a crowded upscale nightclub where Betty is singing on stage. Shortly after the cartoon begins, Bimbo is working frantically in the kitchen as waiter after waiter thrusts his head through the window separating the kitchen from the dining room. Each waiter demands a different dish. Two of them are wearing outdoor-type hats while working indoors, indicating that they are observant Jews. One, notably sporting a nose that looks like a burnt frankfurter and speaking in a thick Jewish accent, says "I vant ham." Bimbo responds by throwing a piece of meat in his face that's marked with the Hebrew letters meaning "kosher" (כשר).

The next waiter, another dog-man with a large canine snout, says "Bagels and bitches, I want knishes, mach' schnell." ("Knishes" are a Jewish dish and "mach' schnell" is German for "Make it quick," indicating the waiter might be an American Jew of German origin.) Bimbo responds by closing the window on him, cutting off his nose. The nose dances around and yells for a couple of seconds and then jumps through the window back into the dining room, presumably to try and reattach itself to its owner's face.

The Fleischers hit their anti-Semitic peak, such as it was, in "Betty Boop's Ups and Downs," released on October 14, 1932. During the Great Depression, millions of Americans, including the character Betty plays in this cartoon, were being forced to sell their homes because they could no longer make their mortgage payments. Betty, apparently unable to afford the house she lives in, leaves it and rides away with Bimbo in a wagon carrying all her household goods.

CHAPTER 1

In the cartoon, the Depression has advanced to such an extent that as Betty's house is advertised for sale, so are millions of others, and so is the Earth itself. At the ensuing auction, the Moon acts as the auctioneer, and other planets vie to purchase Earth. Saturn, portrayed as a big-nosed, behatted, and bearded Orthodox Jew with a heavy Yiddish accent, wins the bidding war. Oddly, although Mars bids 50 and Venus bids 40, Saturn bids 20 and wins. This could possibly be seen as a cartoonish reversal of the real world, but it seems more likely to be an anti-Semitic reference to Jewish stinginess.

After winning with his low bid, Saturn rubs his hands and says "I got 'em! I got deh whole Woyelt [world], I got!" As the Moon asks him repeatedly for the cash, he reaches beneath his beard for his moneybag, and mutters "Here, here, you gonif you." ("Gonif" is a Yiddish term for a disreputable person and often is used as an insult.) Having purchased Earth, Saturn the Jew tries to remove the "For Sale" sign attached to it. He discovers that it's attached to a rope that's connected underground to "The Earth's Magnet," an extremely large one of the U-shaped variety. He tosses the sign aside, pulls up the rope, and says, "I'll pull out gravity from de Oyth and see vuht happin" in a sing-song voice. As he extracts the magnet from the planet and tosses it aside, trees, houses, animals, and people fly into the air, including Betty. (The Fleischers, as was typical for them, took the opportunity to expose more of Betty: as she floats in the air her skirt flies upward due to the absence of gravity.) After seeing that everything on Earth is flying away, Saturn mutters that he "knew I got stuck" with a bad deal just before a hand mysteriously emerges from the Earth and pulls the magnet back into the planet. Every person and every building that had flown away returns to Earth, and the crisis is over. The Fleischers, Democrats as well as Jews, couldn't resist depicting a large elephant falling back to Earth, landing in the middle of the Atlantic and Pacific Oceans and morphing into the Continental United States.

The Betty Boop cartoon "I'll Be Glad When You're Dead, You Rascal You," released November 25, 1932, concentrates most of its mockery on Africans and African Americans. Koko the Clown, however, while being chased by the huge face of Louis Armstrong threatening him musically from the sky, is running so fast that a speedometer magically appears on the clothes covering his rear end. It clocks his speed at "60, 70, 80, 90, 100, ?, !" and then spells "kosher" in Hebrew letters. Experts in gentle ethnic mockery might argue that this is a form of praise, meaning that Jews can run faster than anyone else. On the other hand, because running from an assailant can be seen as cowardly, the scene might be interpreted as meaning that Jews are more cowardly than everyone else. Your choice.

The Fleischers weren't entirely alone in producing cartoons like this during the 1930s. On May 25, 1933, Disney released a cartoon titled "Three Little Pigs" that showed the wolf in the story as a Jewish peddler with a thick Yiddish accent, a large, crooked nose, and a black hat similar to those worn by religious Jews. (In 1948, after knowledge of the Jewish Holocaust had spread around the world, Disney animators replaced this scene with a more acceptable one.)

The Fleischers were never going to push their self-mockery quite this far, but continued pursuing this theme, nevertheless. In their cartoon "Betty Boop's Big Boss," released on June 2, 1933, Betty, a secretary, is being chased and groped by her enormously fat male employer. When his harassment rises to such a level that the police are summoned, the first three patrol vans rolling out of precinct headquarters to answer

Betty's distress call display the sign "Police." The fourth, however, displays the Hebrew letters spelling out "Kosher" once again, this time probably meaning that the cops are rushing to save a Jew—that is, Betty. However, when those Hebrew letters appear, several notes from the Jewish wedding song "Mazel Tov" are heard on the soundtrack, a foreshadowing of the final significant event in this film: after the grossly over-armed and trigger-happy cops attempting to aid Betty destroy most of the office building in which Betty is being harassed by her boss, the cartoon indicates that she and the boss have not only survived his pawing of her and the destruction of the building, but have fallen in love and will soon be married.

Somewhat similar was the cartoon "Betty Boop's Lifeguard," released on July 13, 1934. In this film, a bearded fish with a large nose and a stack of hats balanced precariously on his head—resembling a stereotype of Jewish peddlers of the day—is shown walking on his tail on the bottom of the ocean. Frightened by a sea monster that swims rapidly past him in pursuit of Betty, the peddler drops the clothes he's carrying and runs away.

It's worth remembering that in the 1930s, the Fleischers, along with other Jews and millions of other people around the world, were increasingly aware that a vicious anti-Semite, Adolf Hitler, had become dictator of Germany. They also soon realized that he would allow no one to stand in his way. On June 30, 1934, for instance, Hitler's government carried out an operation later dubbed "The Night of the Long Knives." On that night, his Storm Troopers brutally murdered more than one hundred of his opponents within the Nazi Party, most of them members of the paramilitary organization known as the Brownshirts. Then, on August 2, 1934, Hitler, who sported a small mustache and almost always wore a military uniform, declared himself dictator of Germany and assumed the title of *Fuhrer*, or leader.

In late December of that year, a mustachioed European militarist called Prince Okey Dokey, whose name could be loosely translated as "Prince Sieg Heil," began appearing regularly in Betty's Hollywood comic strip. Like Hitler, Okey Dokey almost never wears anything but a military uniform, complete, as was Hitler's, with boots and military cap. And, apparently unaware that Betty was the child of Jewish parents, Okey Dokey begins courting her. He refuses to abandon this courtship even after Betty, who routinely chases after or attempts to attract men she's interested in, makes it clear she's not interested.

In the very first strip starring Okey Dokey, which appeared on December 24, 1934, Betty tells the director of her upcoming movie that the character is making her "jittery." The director tells her not to worry because the studio has surrounded itself with barbed wire, armed security guards, and boarded-up gates. Okey Dokey gets in anyway. The next day an alarmed studio guard tells Betty that "somebody is bombing the wall" that surrounds the studio. A few seconds later, Okey Dokey struts in proudly through the wall's destroyed section. Somehow anticipating the major role that the German Air Force, the Luftwaffe, would play in battles during World War II, in a cartoon released January 8, 1935, Okey Dokey flies an airplane over the studio wall and lands on the studio grounds inside it. In another cartoon on January 10, he uses an armored car to get in.

Betty keeps discouraging Okey Dokey's attentions, but he keeps sneaking onto the studio grounds in various disguises so he can repeatedly propose to her in person. This approach doesn't seem to be working until Betty's lawyers inform her that her contract with the studio forbids her from listening to proposals of marriage from Okey Dokey or anyone else. Betty refuses to give up her independence to this extent. Even though she's already signed the contract, she demands that Okey Dokey and his attorneys be allowed to argue to her attorneys that in fact, nothing in the contract prevents anyone from proposing to her. The verbal battle royal between the two attorney armies becomes so violent that Okey Dokey, who had helped present his own case to the assembled group, has to be carried out of the room on a stretcher.

Whether or not one considers these cartoons to be anti-Semitic, or trivializing the threat to European Jews, writers Stefan Kanfer, Ann Douglas, and others have argued that all this mocking and teasing stemmed from the fact that the Fleischers, many of the employees of their studio, and Betty all were New York Jews, and that New York was, and is, home to approximately 1.1 million Jews, who belong to the largest Jewish community outside Israel. As if to emphasize this point, when the Fleischer operation eventually relocated, it moved not to the West Coast but to Miami, Florida, the retirement destination of millions of New York Jews. The largely non-Jewish Disney Studios, of course, was headquartered in Burbank, where it remains today.

2

INTRODUCING
BETTY BOOP

Betty Boop started her on-screen cartoon life as a girlfriend for Bimbo the dog-man, an already existing Fleischer Studios cartoon star, whom the Fleischers had created as an answer to Walt Disney's Mickey Mouse. (The Fleischers were shrewd to pick a doglike person to star with Betty rather than a mouse, which had been Disney's choice. Very few Americans love mice but millions of American families in the 1930s owned and loved dogs.)

In any case, Bimbo was a pretty advanced mutt. Although clearly a canine, he wore clothes, spoke English, played musical instruments with his forepaws, walked on his hind legs, and otherwise acted completely human. Nevertheless, as a dog-man he needed a partly doggy girlfriend.

The cartoons in which Bimbo's interest in women is noted also show that the Fleischer brothers, Max, Dave, and Lou, were fans of the era's popular musicians. (Lou headed the Music Department at Fleischer

Studios.) In the cartoon "Hot Dog," released on March 29, 1930, in which Bimbo starred and in which Betty did not appear, Bimbo was shown out driving and trying to pick up women walking on the sidewalk. At the time, "hot dog" was slang for "attractive woman."

Appropriately enough, considering this quest of Bimbo's, his name had two different meanings at the beginning of his cartoon career. When he was first dubbed "Bimbo," that word meant a tough guy, or a criminal. Soon after Bimbo's character began appearing on the screen, however, "bimbo" came to mean a promiscuous woman. Whether or not this shift in meaning was partly prodded by Bimbo's relentless on-screen pursuits, it underscored his interest in women.

(The title of this cartoon also may have been a subtle Fleischer reference to the competition between Mickey Mouse and Bimbo. Their rivalry had begun the previous year when Mickey's first cartoon, "The Karnival Kid," was released on May 23, 1929, and "Hot dogs! Hot dogs!" were Mickey's first on-screen comments in it. He wasn't referring to women, however, since he'd been speaking these words while selling frankfurters at a carnival.)

In "Hot Dog," Bimbo soon focuses on one woman he thinks might be attractive. When she turns out to be ugly and mostly toothless, he tries to escape her by tunneling under the pavement in his car. That move attracts police attention, but unaware of their official interest, Bimbo then focuses on a bosomy young woman roller-skating down the street, lures her into his car, and attempts to romance her. Unfortunately for Bimbo, the young woman isn't interested and soon escapes on her skates. He pursues her on foot but then is nabbed by the cops and hauled into court for digging holes in the public street with his car.

Once in court, Bimbo escapes a penalty by producing a banjo out of nowhere, dancing a few steps, and singing portions of "St. Louis Blues," a song about unrequited love. The song, strictly speaking, is unrelated to the offense for which Bimbo's been arrested, but he obviously hopes to gain the court's sympathy by singing it as part of his defense. The Fleischers apparently thought "St. Louis Blues" would be particularly appropriate to this cartoon because it deals with unrequited love. The male judge and the all-male jury listen intently, and then dance to Bimbo's performance. Naturally, he leaves court unpenalized.

While Bimbo has no further legal problems that day, his sexual predicament remains obvious: How many women want a dog, or even a dog-man, for a lover? Maybe some novelty seekers, but they're hard to find.

The cartoon version of Betty was created to fill this need. Early one morning in 1930, Dave Fleischer told animator Grim Natwick to design a girl dog who would costar with Bimbo in a cartoon to be titled "Dizzy Dishes." Natwick was told that the new character, as yet unnamed, would be singing a "boop-oop-a-doop" song similar to those sung by Helen Kane. Fleischer also handed Natwick a picture of Kane.

Having been told to create a female dog for Bimbo, Natwick drew a poodle named Betty who walked on four legs and sported a pelvic-shaped human head

Photograph of Grim Natwick from the November 1969 issue of *Cartoonist PROfiles*. COURTESY INTERNET ARCHIVE.

Helen Kane in a still from the 1929 film *Sweetie*.

complete with long dangling ears, canine jowls, and a button nose. Above Betty's ears, however, he gifted her with one of the popular feminine hairstyles of the day, singer and actress Helen Kane's spit curls.

Fleischer took one look at Natwick's outlandish creation and ordered him to turn the character's body into that of a woman. Natwick immediately ripped the head he'd created off its doggy torso and perched it on the body of a human woman, Betty Boop. "I put cute, feminine legs on her," Natwick said later. The woman he'd drawn was now all girl, at least from the tips of her toes to the top of her torso.

The problem began just above her shoulders. She sported a doggy-type nose, doggy ears, doggy jowls, and no neck. Why Natwick decided not to provide Betty with a neck has been lost in the annals of animation history. Many of her subsequent animators complained that it was hard for her to move realistically from place to place with no neck to steer herself by. Her head stayed in one position while her legs moved all over the place.

This was also a problem for many of Betty's fans, because it meant that she rarely, if ever, kissed any of her on-screen admirers. There's a reason kissing is sometimes called "necking": it's very difficult to do the former without using the latter, and Betty just didn't have the equipment. She definitely expressed her affection for men, but almost always in other ways.

Natwick's fellow animators would eventually solve Betty's neck problem. They perfected the animation of Betty in profile so her cartoon head would move in conjunction with the rest of her body, even though she had no neck.

Betty, making her first appearance in "Dizzy Dishes," sings to Bimbo, who is working in the restaurant as a waiter and a chef. "I have to have lovin'," Betty sings to Bimbo from the stage. "I have to have you."

The lyrics were from the song "I Have to Have You," written by Leo Robin and performed by Helen Kane in the 1929 musical comedy film *Pointed Heels*, in which she costarred with William Powell and Fay Wray. What Kane sang in her movie was "Sometimes I get so blue waiting for you to take me. I can't go on like this!" Betty, while bending forward and staring straight at Bimbo, sings "I'm so blue, waiting for you, to [indecipherable] me. I can't go on like this." The Fleischers just couldn't bring themselves to show Betty asking a dog-man to "take" her.

Betty then flips up the back of her dress several times in a way that inevitably evokes the position that dogs, and presumably some dog-men, use to consummate their relationships. Bimbo certainly seems to get the message. He responds to Betty's attentions by enthusiastically dancing in place and accompanying her on a ukulele. He also sings her chosen phrase, "boop-boop-a-doop" right back at her. All this would seem quite promising, except that Bimbo leaves the premises soon after this exchange, apparently having completely forgotten about Betty. Some dog-men are like that.

Audiences didn't forget about Betty, however. In fact, they reacted favorably to Betty and her no-holds-barred approach to romance. As a result, the Fleischers made Betty their major cartoon star and demoted Bimbo to spending the rest of his career playing a supporting role as Betty's love interest. But what a role!

At this point, the animated Betty, along with her canine nose and jowls, still sported long cocker spaniel–type ears that were not only doggy-shaped but displayed no visible earlobes or earlike canals. A few months later, however, someone at Fleischer Studios realized how odd she looked. "Somebody changed those ears into earrings," Natwick said. "Maybe I did. We thought that as long as she looked like a girl anyways, let's just make her all girl."

By the time Betty's cartoon "Any Rags" was released on January 4, 1932, her doggy ears had become long earrings, and her doggy nose had become a small human nose. When her cartoon "Minnie the Moocher" appeared on March 11 of that year, Betty's doggy jowls also were missing. Except for having no neck, Betty's character now looked like a real girl.

Previously, several cartoons had heavily implied that dog-eared Betty and Bimbo were having sex; with Betty now indisputably human, that would no longer be suggested. The fact that Bimbo was part dog and Betty was all woman meant that, as Prof. Mark Langer of Carleton

Betty's features had become more conventional by the 1932 cartoon "Any Rags?" PHOTOFEST.

University has put it, "Betty's relationship with Bimbo was more than a little strange; it was a lot strange."

Natwick had dressed Betty in a very short skirt and adorned one of her legs with a garter, making her the first fully human, and fully female, animated cartoon character ever. "Eight years of art school and night classes, drawing what must have been thousands of naked models, taught me a little bit about the female body," Natwick told an interviewer. "I knew all the sexy angles and shapes, from the turn of the ankle to the shape of the heel of her shoe to where her waist belonged." Later, he led the team of three animators who drew Snow White for Walt Disney.

When Natwick decided to accentuate Betty's human femininity by giving her provocative cleavage and bouncing breasts, the real Betty Boop cartoon character was born. "She was an alluring little sexpot," another one of Betty's animators, Shamus Culhane, recalled in his 1986 autobiography, *Talking Animals and Other People*. Natwick understood Betty's appeal better than anyone. As he told author Jeff Lenberg, "Although she was never vulgar or obscene, Betty was a suggestion you could spell in three letters: S-E-X."

Author Jake Austen sums up Betty's sexpot appeal: "With her thick gartered thighs, high heels, and cleavage, Betty, pre–Hays Code, was always the object of her costars' (and the audience's) desires. She would have her clothes fall off, revealing sexy lingerie, her skirt blown upward, her body revealed by a strong backlight, and on at least two occasions, perform a topless hula dance. Betty is routinely chased by every race, species, and inanimate object, from fish to fossils."

Consider the cartoon "Bimbo's Express," released on August 22, 1931. On arriving at Betty's door to begin helping her move, Bimbo knocks and Betty, only half-dressed while trimming her toenails, tells him she can't answer the door right away because she is wearing a nightie. Bimbo's immediate response is, "I'll wait 'til you take it off." Betty, however, realizing that Bimbo is accompanied by several other moving men, puts on a dress rather than exhibit herself. Bimbo continues to praise her beauty as the crew packs up her belongings. The two lovers then sit close together on the front seat of the horse-drawn moving van as they ride off into the sunset.

To nobody's surprise, the apartment Betty has moved into, as portrayed in the cartoon "Minding the Baby," released on September 28, 1931, is separated from Bimbo's by only an alley. Like many other similarly situated lovers in those days, the two of them exchange notes via a clothesline connecting the two apartments. The propinquity of their apartments would have been quite convenient for lovemaking, except that Bimbo is sharing his with his mother and baby brother, and Betty is sharing hers with her mother.

When both mothers go out to shop, however, Betty tries to lure Bimbo over to her place by spelling out, in a little ditty she sings to him across the alley, exactly what she wants Bimbo to do: play "Dad" while she played "Mom." From a little girl this might have seemed innocent, but Betty was wearing a sexy dress and makeup and was obviously of age. Soon overcome with lust, Bimbo propels himself via clothesline over to Betty's place. Once over there, however, he loses his nerve, and rather than play "la jeu d'amour," as the French might say, he and Betty play "the game of jump rope."

Of course, Betty was hardly the only on-screen character who was thinking about, or moving toward, having sex in the 1930s. Movie companies turned to sex and violence in the Depression era as a way of bringing in the paying public. Mae West, Jean Harlow, and other female film stars of the time were known for their sexy talk and general sex appeal, and Betty was the first cartoon character to mimic them. She also could expand upon her sexuality, or enact it, in weirder ways than any real woman could.

Obviously, Betty's cartoons were aimed at adults, not at children, and in fact they were usually shown on the same bill with feature films aimed at adults. The adults at which these cartoons were aimed seemed to enjoy them immensely. Theater owners who played cartoons before their featured film was shown were often motivated to play the same Betty Boop cartoon twice in a row because their audience clapped so loudly, and for so long, after the cartoon's first showing.

As the animated Betty began starring in more and more cartoons, the basic elements of her personality, including her desire for sex, her independent way of existing in the world, and her aggressive and successful careerism, began to become obvious.

Betty soon became so popular that she was touted as the Fleischers' most important property, causing them to bill her quite accurately as "The Queen of the Animated Screen." Having previously de-animalized Betty's features, the Fleischers and their animators now worked to expand her sexual opportunities. They decided she should try to attract fully human men, and thus become much more like the great majority of American women. This was certainly understandable.

What was less understandable was that in many cartoons Betty kept pursuing Bimbo romantically, and he pursued her, even after she became fully human. In the carefully chosen words of author Karl Cohen, Betty's transformation into a complete human "did not stop her animators from suggesting that her relationship with Bimbo went beyond the affection a person has for a pet."

Now, however, numerous other non-doggy humans were in competition for her affection with Bimbo the dog-man. In the cartoon "Mask-A-Raid," released on November 9, 1931, Betty and Bimbo both attend a masked costume party set in a medieval court. Betty is playing the Queen, and Bimbo is leading the band playing at the event. At one point Betty stops her royal parade, bares one shoulder, and shimmies right in front of Bimbo. She keeps flirting with him later in the cartoon by fingering her décolletage and exposing her stockinged gams up to and above the tops of her nylons.

Both Bimbo and an old man who fancies Betty can hardly help but notice her come-ons. To distract his potential rival, Bimbo doffs a mask and starts singing the song "Where Do You Worka, John?"

This aria mocked the accents of the Italian immigrants who worked on the Delaware Lackawanna Railroad. Also known as "The Delaware Lackawanna Song," the tune was composed by Salvatore Guaragna in 1926. (Guaragna also composed the song "I Only Have Eyes for You," which Betty and her soon-to-be boyfriend Freddy would sing as "I Only Have Ice for You" in a later Betty production.) Born in Brooklyn, Guaragna eventually grew tired of spelling his name to people over and over and changed it to Harry Warren. He wrote or cowrote over eight hundred songs between 1918 and 1981, many of which were used in films and cartoons, including "There Will Never Be Another You," "Forty-Second Street," "We're In the Money," "Lullaby of Broadway," "Serenade in Blue," "Jeepers Creepers," "You're Getting to Be a Habit with Me," "That's Amore," and "Chattanooga Choo-Choo." In retrospect, it's amazing that this one guy wrote so many classic American songs.

Guaragna changing his name to a standard American one, and "The Delaware Lackawanna Song" itself, both resulted from the massive immigration of Italians to the United States during the late nineteenth and early twentieth centuries. This flood of immigrants was a result of the unification of Italy during the 1860s, which resulted in an improvement in economic conditions in southern Italy, which in turn led to an overpopulation of the Italian peninsula. Of all the immigrants to the United States from 1920 to 1930, 551,000, or 12 percent, were Italians. Because many of them were olive-skinned Catholics who didn't speak English, or spoke it poorly, they were often discriminated against and mocked. Many Americans even feared that the mostly Catholic Italians would pay allegiance to the pope rather than to the United States and its leaders.

In any case, in the "Mask-A-Raid" cartoon, the old man's shock or glee at hearing Bimbo sing a song making fun of immigrants while he himself is ogling Betty lasts only a few seconds. Despite Betty's obvious preference for Bimbo, the old man immediately begins competing for her physically by grabbing one of her arms. Bimbo grabs the other one in response, and the two men pull Betty back and forth between them while each of them yells, "She's mine!" They tug at her so vigorously that her skirt rises above her waist, revealing her undergarments.

For better or for worse, Betty's animators would continue to expose, or allow other characters to fondle, various parts of her body. In the cartoon titled "Dizzy Red Riding Hood," released on December 12, 1931, Betty's dress flies up above her waist and is pulled down by a nearby tree.

Later in the same cartoon, Betty, playing the lead character, visits her grandmother only to discover that Bimbo, disguised as a wolf, has taken her place. Taking advantage of Betty's surprise, Bimbo puts one of his hands on her chest.

In "Boop-Oop-A-Doop," released on January 1, 1932, Betty dances and sings in a circus while wearing a two-piece bathing suit and balancing on a highwire. Unfortunately for her, the only admirer with immediate access to her person is the grossly fat and mustachioed circus ringmaster. He follows her to her dressing tent after her performance, rubs his hands up and down her legs, and threatens to fire her if she doesn't give in.

Singing "Don't take my boop-boop-a-doop away," Betty fights back both verbally and physically. But she is much smaller than he is, and her struggles seem futile until Koko the Clown enters the fight and vanquishes Betty's assailant. He asks Betty if the ringmaster had forced

A lecherous ringmaster pursues Betty in "Boop-Oop-a-Doop" (1932).

himself on her, but she tells him the big brute was unsuccessful. "He couldn't take my boop-boop-a-doop away," she says. What she meant by "boop-boop-a-doop" had become fairly obvious by this point.

3

THE MEN—AND WOMEN—BEHIND BETTY

Grim Natwick, despite having created Betty Boop, would pass up a major opportunity in 1939, when studio president Max Fleischer asked him to animate her for her eighty-seventh Fleischer cartoon, "Musical Mountaineers," released on May 12 of that year. He sugarcoated the work assignment by telling Natwick how great an asset Betty had been to the studio over the years, and how much he'd appreciated Natwick's work with her.

Fleischer then offered Natwick the rights to Betty's character once her last cartoon was released. Natwick, apparently uninterested, never followed up on this offer. Years later, when Natwick heard that Fleischer had sold the rights to reproduce Betty to King Features Syndicate for a big pile of old-fashioned money, Natwick sued. He had no evidence that Fleischer had ever made him such an offer, however, and never was able to cash in on his greatest creation.

(Nonetheless, Natwick, who passed away in 1990, would be immortalized long after his death when his name and occupation were used as a model for the "Grim Matchstick" character in the popular Cuphead video game, which itself was inspired by the animation styles of the 1920s and 1930s, including Fleischer studio cartoons.)

Natwick may have first drawn Betty Boop, but he was not the only animator to work on her cartoons. In fact, Betty's personality traits, all of which were on display in her cartoons, were hardly surprising, since her personal history resembled that of Shamus Culhane, one of her most prolific animators. Significantly, both Betty and Culhane had had problems with their fathers. Culhane's problem was symbolized by his own first name. An American of Irish heritage, he'd been given the name James at birth, but later rejected it and used its Irish equivalent, Shamus, because his father, also named James, had abandoned the family when Shamus was sixteen. His father's departure had forced Shamus to drop out of school to help support his mother and his two siblings. The Betty of the "Minnie the Moocher" cartoon similarly dislikes and rejects her own overbearing father.

In addition to Culhane and Natwick, Betty was drawn by a group of young, sexually aggressive, and almost exclusively male Fleischer Studio animators who worked alongside them. For much of Betty's career, the scripts for the cartoons, although roughed out by Dave Fleischer, were mostly written by the animators themselves. Most aspects of Betty's cartoon personality flowed naturally from the lives adopted by Culhane, Natwick, and the other young men who animated her, most of whom were in their late teens or early twenties. They'd previously turned over most of their salaries to their parents, but now they were relatively well paid and living away from home for

The Autobiography of One of
Animation's Legendary Figures

TALKING ANIMALS AND OTHER PEOPLE

Shamus Culhane

Shamus Culhane shared memories of the Fleischer days in his
1986 autobiography *Talking Animals and Other People*.

the first time as Prohibition ended and the Great Depression drove
rents through the floor.

These low rents, along with a natural desire for sexual and other
freedoms, inspired them to move one by one during 1930 into a brown-
stone rooming house on 44th Street in Manhattan that they almost
completely took over. (The only woman living in the building was

Edith Vernick, a Fleischer studio department head.) Not only were they working near wide-open Times Square, they lived near there as well.

Inspired by their proximity to the bawdy side of life, "the young male animators gathered for a weekly bout of sex, drinking and bridge every Saturday night," Culhane wrote, "with a bevy of whores from a local bordello. The whores were very good bridge players, in addition to their other attributes, and the games, both horizontal and vertical, usually continued all night."

Soon, standard Monday-morning discussions among the young men consisted mostly of boasts about how many times they'd scored, and with which girl, over the weekend. They were becoming urban provocateurs and couldn't help but make Betty one too. However, their sexual mores were somewhat primitive. As Culhane wrote, like most young males at the time, "when the boys talked about sex, there was the usual dichotomy of mothers and sisters being good, and all other women being fair game." As far as these animators were concerned, women, in their relationships with men, were able to do only two things: give them sex or not. Romance was never even considered. This attitude strongly influenced the conduct of their creation, Ms. Boop.

Culhane tried to encapsulate the young animators' attitude toward women by writing about an uncle of his who visited him in New York City several times a year to go to Minsky's Burlesque. Culhane would accompany him. "He would sit tensely and watch the big breasts wobble," Culhane wrote, "and lean forward excitedly as women with incredibly huge buttocks ground languidly down the runway." On one occasion, Culhane took him to Ziegfeld's burlesque theater instead of Minsky's. The female performers at Ziegfeld's were gorgeous dancers in perfect shape who wore glamorous outfits. His uncle "sat very quietly,"

Culhane wrote, "as the six-foot Amazons in sequins and peacock tails pirouetted and strutted around the stage. When we came out of the theater, I asked him how he liked the show. 'Shit,' he growled. 'Next time let's go back to Minsky's.' I had taken him beyond the range of his fantasies."

Given the animators' crude attitudes toward women, Culhane noted, "There was no possibility of a [cartoon] story being written where Betty Boop used her charms in a light, flirtatious manner. Betty was a 'good' girl with a hymen like a boiler plate, and her sex life would never be more than a series of attacks on that virginity by unpleasant characters with heavy hands."

And so it was, at least for a while. In many of her cartoons, Betty rarely seemed to progress beyond fighting off sexual aggressors or flirting, to no avail, with men to whom she was attracted. In the opinion of her young male animators, the men courting Betty wanted sex or nothing, and, like them, were uninterested in marriage.

Natwick, Betty's creator, lived to be one hundred years old but never broke completely with his youthful sexual attitudes. When fans of Betty would ask him to draw pictures of Betty during the 1970s and 1980s, he'd draw her in the nude.

Although most of Betty's male animators would now perhaps be dubbed anti-feminists, Betty's existence as a cartoon character, along with some help from Culhane, made Fleischer employee Lillian Friedman America's first female animator. While the animated Betty was never segregated from men, the two female cartoonists at Fleischer's, Friedman and Edith Vernick, were. Workers in the all-male Animation Department made the key drawings for cartoons while Vernick was the director of, and Friedman worked in, what was called the Inbetweener

Department, where they made less crucial sketches to go in between the key drawings.

Noticing that Friedman was very skilled at her job, Culhane, who was the head animator, announced one day in 1933 that he was going to move her into the Animation Department. His intention was to coordinate his work more effectively with hers and thus produce better completed cartoons. An uproar resulted. "The animators didn't want any fucking women in their fucking department," Culhane said. In fact, before Friedman had become a Fleischer employee, she'd applied for an animator job with Disney Studios but had been told that woman were never hired for that position.

Culhane, advanced for his time, argued that talent, not gender, should be the deciding factor in job placement. He made no headway, however. So, finally, he proposed that all qualified inbetweeners, male and female, complete the same animation test but submit their drawings anonymously. Then he let Willard Bowsky, the animator who'd most vociferously opposed Friedman's promotion, pick out the best result from the unsigned work. When Bowsky unwittingly chose Friedman's drawing, Friedman was given the job and became America's first female studio animator.

(In addition to his misogyny, Bowsky was also said to be a vociferous anti-Semite, even though he worked for the Fleischers. Somewhat ironically, he was killed in action while serving in the US Army fighting the Nazis in Europe. He was posthumously awarded the Purple Heart and the Silver Star and is buried in France.)

Friedman's promotion turned out to be such a breakthrough for American women that it resulted in newspaper publicity throughout the country. (Lotte Reiniger, later a well-known film director, had

Lillian Friedman not only was the first woman to draw Betty, but she is also widely regarded as the first American female animator.

begun working as an animator in Germany in 1918, so there was no similar publicity outside the United States.) A United Press story that circulated throughout America marveled that Friedman, "a young woman, aged only 22 . . . has proved that she can draw Betty Boop and Popeye [another Fleischer character] as well, and as consistently, as any of the better masculine artists." The article went on to state that "Max

Fleischer, father of screen cartoons . . . found it difficult to believe that this conservative girl, who had never even joined in office conversation during the three years she has been on his lesser personnel pay roll, had actually made the grade."

The story didn't mention that although the Fleischer animators were generally paid more than the inbetweeners, Friedman's new contract with the studio provided her with a starting salary of only $30 a week, plus a raise of five dollars a week every year for four years. This may not seem to have been all that bad for the 1930s, but her male fellow animators were being paid $100 a week with a raise to $125 a week in the second year.

Despite this salary disparity, Friedman stayed at the company until 1939, helping Betty rise to stardom. She animated numerous Betty Boop cartoons and many other Fleischer productions, although she received screen credit for only six cartoons during her lifetime. (This was not necessarily because of misogyny: a controversial Fleischer policy allowed only the names of one director and two animators to be cited at the beginning of each cartoon. There were usually more than two animators involved, however.)

Friedman's promotion to animator did shake up the American cartoon world a bit. Only one year later, female animator Laverne Harding went to work for Walter Lantz Productions in Los Angeles. Even in 1936, however, more than three years after Friedman and Harding had begun their successful careers, a promotional booklet issued by Paramount Studios, the company that distributed the Fleischer Studio's cartoons, stated that "Nobody knows just why, but women generally are not successful as cartoon animators." Two years after that, in 1938, in response to a job application from a Mary V. Ford, a Walt

Disney executive wrote that "Women do not do any of the creative work in connection with preparing the cartoons for the screen, as that work is performed entirely by young men." For this reason, Ford wrote, "girls are not considered for the training school . . . The only work open to women consists of tracing the characters on clear celluloid sheets with India ink and filling in the tracings on the reverse side with paint according to directions."

Naturally, of course, the actors who gave Betty Boop her voice were always women. Although Max Fleischer would later testify under oath that Betty's personality and singing style had appeared fully formed in his imagination and was in no way an imitation of Helen Kane, the first woman to provide Betty's voice was Margie Hines, who had been selected after winning one of hundreds of Helen Kane Impersonation Competitions (also known as "Boop-Oop-A-Doop" contests, evoking Kane's singing style) being held throughout the country.

Hines provided Betty's voice in Betty's first two cartoons, "Dizzy Dishes" and "Mysterious Mose," both released in 1930, and "Betty Co-Ed," released in 1931. She also voiced Betty again at the end of the decade in several cartoons including "Rhythm on the Reservation," which was released in 1939. These were only bookend events, however, that bracketed the more publicized achievements of Hines's life.

Betty's fellow Fleischer cartoon character, Popeye, had a well-known girlfriend named Olive Oyl, and between her two boops as Betty's voice, Hines rose to greater fame by becoming the voice of Olive Oyl. In 1938, she married Jack Mercer, who was providing Popeye's voice. "Popeye and Olive Oyl Marry," screamed the headlines. The human couple's wedding, held in Ft. Lauderdale, Florida, naturally featured a breakfast of spinach. "Blow me down," Mercer shouted after

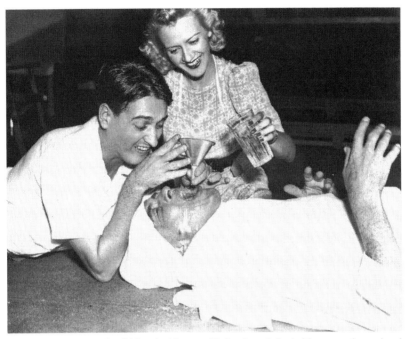

Publicity photograph of Margie Hines with husband Jack Mercer, who voiced Popeye the Sailor. They are shown here pouring water into the mouth of fellow voice actor Pinto Colvig as part of a recording for the 1939 Fleischer production *Gulliver's Travels.*

the wedding, "but Olive is a pertikiller bride. She won't let me smoke me tabacky in the parlor!" Popeye had let Mercer borrow his voice for the occasion. Hines went on to provide Olive Oyl's voice in the 1943 cartoon, "The Marry-Go-Round," but the title of this cartoon was prophetic: Hines and Mercer divorced in 1950.

Another of Betty's voice providers, Bonnie Poe, made history in 1933 by voicing Betty on the radio for the first time when Betty starred on the NBC radio show *Betty Boop Fables.* Like Hines, Poe had voiced Popeye and Olive Oyl in several productions before lending Betty her voice in fourteen cartoons, including "Betty in Blunderland," "Betty Boop's Rise to Fame," and "Betty Boop's Lifeguard," all released in

1934. Poe then rose to the top by carrying Betty's fame from cartoons into movies for the first time. She supplied Betty not only with a voice, but with a real human body. In a short skit in the popular 1933 film *Hollywood on Parade*, Poe wore a low-cut top, sang and looked like Betty, and let herself be accosted by Bela Lugosi. Playing Dracula, Lugosi bent her way over backward, threatened her throat with his gleaming teeth, and told her "You've booped your last boop." Poe screamed, and the scene ended.

Somewhat less impressive, at least physically, was Betty's next voice provider, Little Ann Little. Born Ann Rothschild, Little Ann first rose to prominence by winning a Paramount Pictures contest to find a girl with a squeaky voice, the sine qua non for Betty's voicers. As her professional name indicates, Little Ann was indeed little, being only four feet ten inches tall and weighing only seventy-six pounds. On the other hand, her diminutive height made her look more like the real Betty than her competitors did.

After starting in show business in 1925 as a member of the Greenwich Village Follies chorus, Little displayed a lot more business moxie than some of the other voicers. An early TV star, for a while she hosted her own program on the NBC Network. Later, Little began touring the nation's department stores with former Fleischer Studios artist Pauline Comanor. She would pose as Betty and then Comanor would draw her and hand out the completed drawings to the wide-eyed children and their mothers who'd gathered to watch. In tribute to Betty, Comanor and Little would then finish their presentation by "boop-boop-a-dooping" in unison. Little also had studied to become a minister and was ordained in the Unity Church of Christianity. "Betty Boop Studying for the Ministry," one newspaper headline informed its readers. Little kept on preaching the gospel until she died at age seventy-one.

Betty voicer Harriet Lee also showed a lot of gumption, starting her career by selling sheet music in a Chicago retail store to pay for voice lessons. She later became a singer on numerous CBS-TV programs and the Radio Queen of the 1939 World's Fair, finally capping off her career by becoming the voice coach for movie stars Janet Leigh and Dorothy Lamour. Lee only aided Betty in one cartoon, however: "The Bum Bandit." Her main task in that film was to voice the song "I'm Dangerous Nan McGrew," which was sung on-screen by Betty. This ended Lee's booping career because she sang the song in her own style rather than in Betty's inimitable squeak, which irritated the Fleischers.

(Later, vocalist Catherine Wright also lent her voice to Betty for a radio show or two but never contributed to any of Betty's cartoons. Betty's other voicers in various productions included Angelia, Alex Borstein, LeAnne Broas, Didi Conn, Shannon Cullem, Sandy Fox, Michelle Goquen, Heather Halley, Alice Hamada, Lani Minella, Nicole Van Giesen, Sara Stiles, and Kat Wright.)

The departures of Lee and Wright set the scene for Betty's most popular voicer, the magnificent Mae Questel, who looked and sounded exactly like Betty and would provide Betty with a voice for most of her cartoon career. Reviewers agreed that Questel brought a wonderful combination of sweetness and sauciness to the role. Questel voiced Betty in 1931 in the "Betty Co-Ed" cartoon and went on to give Betty her voice for most of her cartoons through 1939.

Born in New York City in 1908, Questel was raised in the Bronx. Her Orthodox Jewish parents urged her to pursue a teaching career.

Betty's most popular voicer was Mae Questel, pictured here with Max Fleischer.
PHOTOFEST.

She began to do so at a teachers' college, but her sorority sisters, aware of her acting talent, entered her without her knowledge in a Helen Kane impersonation contest. Although surprised at her sudden candidacy for this role, Questel took the trouble to observe Kane onstage beforehand, something the other contestants had not managed to do.

This shrewd move by Questel and her obvious acting talent allowed her to deliver a dead-on impersonation that not only won the contest, but also earned her a paid performer's slot on the Radio-Keith-Orpheum (RKO) vaudeville circuit.

Questel's RKO act, logically enough, consisted of impersonations of celebrities such as Fannie Brice, Marlene Dietrich, Rudy Vallee, Maurice Chevalier and, of course, Helen Kane. When Max Fleischer saw Questel's on-stage performance, he immediately hired her as Betty's new voice. Fleischer must have been really impressed by Questel's on-stage impersonation of Kane. A year or two after witnessing it, he memorialized it in Betty's cartoon "Stopping the Show," released on August 12, 1932. The cartoon features Betty, using Questel's voice, imitating Questel as a vaudeville headliner doing imitations of Fanny Brice, Maurice Chevalier, and others.

Questel had first voiced Betty the year before, however, when she provided Betty the voice in which Betty sang "You're Driving Me Crazy" on stage in a large legitimate theater in the cartoon "Silly Scandals," released May 21, 1931. Betty had added to the appeal of her on-stage performance by wearing an even shorter skirt than usual and allowing the top of her dress to dip while she sang, thus revealing a sexy black bra. Bimbo the dog-man, in the audience, was mightily impressed, as were numerous other viewers, most of them male.

Although Questel enjoyed voicing Betty, she was so talented that she also played and voiced other characters during various stage and radio performances. A year later, however, she returned to voice Betty in "Minnie the Moocher," the 1932 cartoon that began with Betty interacting with her parents. From then on until 1939, Questel was Betty all the way, voicing the rest of the ninety Betty Boop cartoons produced during that period. Her unmistakable New York accent became synonymous with Betty's.

Questel not only voiced Betty, she also melded her own personality with Betty's, telling author Leslie Cabarga that she "lived" the part. "It took me a long time to lower my voice and get away from the character," she said, once she finally stopped performing Betty. She had become so identified with Betty, in fact, that when the Fleischer studios moved from New York to Florida in the late 1930s and Questel declined to go along, Max and Dave Fleischer declared that Betty's career was over.

Even forty-eight years later, however, Questel was still so attached to Betty that she returned to the screen in 1988 to voice Betty one more time in Betty's big comeback movie, *Who Framed Roger Rabbit*. Perhaps reinspired by this Hollywood success, Questel went on to live another ten years and died at age ninety in 1998.

4

MUSIC AND THE CARTOONS

Betty's use of the Helen Kane song "I Have to Have You" in her "Dizzy Dishes" cartoon was just the beginning of her on-screen musical career. Betty and her voicers sang a great many songs during their careers, and at least eight of those songs were written just for her.

Among Betty's songwriters was Sammy Timberg, who wrote one song about her, named "Sweet Betty," and another tune that Betty sang, "Don't Take My Boop-Boop-A-Doop Away." Timberg also wrote several other songs for Betty and/or other characters in six of her cartoons: "A Language All My Own," "Be Human," "Keep a Little Song Handy," "A Little Soap and Water," "Grampy's House," and "Little Pal."

Although Timberg was the Fleischer Studios music director, he couldn't be as loyal to Betty as he seemed to want to be, since his employers required him to write songs for Popeye as well. Later, Timberg would also write songs for the nine Superman cartoons the Fleischers produced in 1941 and 1942.

Other composers came forward to write songs for Betty, and numerous women were available to sing the songs for her as well as be her voice. They included some of her professional voicers plus Camilla Bard, Cheryl Chase, Marie Danielle, Victoria D'Orazi, Melissa Fahn, Desiree Goyette, Rose Marie, and Sue Raney.

At least one of these women sang a Betty Boop song on her own. Japanese singer Alice Hamada was backed by the Columbia Jazz Band and recorded a tune for Betty titled "Tweet Tweet Tweet" in 1937. While it's certain that the war between the United States and Japan that began in December 1941 killed Hamada's American sales, it's difficult to determine the popularity of any of the songs that were sung by Betty via her various voicers. That's because until July 1941, sales of recorded music were not systematically charted.

Nevertheless, Betty often used songs that had been originally sung and/or composed by others as a means of seduction. In the cartoon "Betty Boop's Big Boss," released on June 2, 1933, she answers an advertisement that declares "Girl Wanted—Female Preferred." When Betty shows up for an interview and the boss asks her "What can you do?" Betty replies with a flirty female office worker's version of the 1919 song "You'd Be Surprised," written by Irving Berlin. To perform it, she uses a voice provided by Little Ann Little to sing such lines as: "I'm not so good in a crowd but when you get me alone, you'd be surprised."

Considering this incredibly obvious come-on, it surprises no one when Betty gets the job, but both the boss and the audience are astonished when she then fights back, successfully, against the boss's sexual advances. Despite the disappointment suffered by Betty's lecherous boss, this song remained popular for years. Although Betty sang her version in 1933, the song was recorded by Mae Questel in 1940 and by

Kathy Linden in 1958, with Linden's version reaching Number 50 on the *Billboard* Pop Chart. With Betty, the only way to go was up.

It was at this point that the Fleischer brothers decided to save script-writing time by not only using popular tunes in Betty's cartoons but using them to provide the underlying plots for those same cartoons. They started by basing the Betty Boop cartoon "Barnacle Bill the Sailor," which was released on August 30, 1930, on the traditional ditty titled "Barnacle Bill." This song, which describes the alleged antics of a nineteenth-century sailor named William Bernard, was first recorded in 1928. It was rerecorded by Bix Beiderbecke and Hoagy Carmichael two months before the Fleischers released the cartoon. The traditional versions of the song are semi-obscene, but the recorded versions and the Fleischer cartoon version of the tune were partly sanitized. The underlying meaning of the song remains evident, however.

In keeping with the spirit of both the song and the cartoon built around it, Betty wears low-cut outfits in this film that definitely clash with her long doggy ears. When Barnacle, played by Bimbo, visits Betty in her apartment, she wastes no time before asking him if he'd lie down with her. The Fleischers had somehow rigged Betty's skirt to second this suggestion by rising up to her waist, although she quickly pulls it down again. Barnacle, who probably doesn't need such an obvious come-on to go into action, replies, "You're the gal for me," and the couple pulls down the shade. Outside, Betty's neighbors whisper, wink at each other, and point knowingly at her apartment.

As soon as the shade is raised, the neighbors can see Betty and Barnacle—playing checkers in Betty's living room. No one is fooled, however, partly because Barnacle remains shirtless, revealing tattooed pictures of women all over his exposed upper body. Before he leaves,

Betty implores him to stay, but he replies, "Never again, I'll come no more, I'm Barnacle Bill the Sailor."

All of this lined up perfectly with the lyrics of the traditional song, which include the words

"I got me a wife in every port," Said Barnacle Bill the Sailor.
"The handsome gals is what I court,"
Said Barnacle Bill the Sailor.
"With my false heart and flattering tongue
I courts 'em all both old and young, I courts 'em all, but marries none,"
Said Barnacle Bill the Sailor.

With Betty still hungry for true love, and still sporting doggie ears, the Fleischers used Betty as Bimbo-bait only four months later, on December 26, 1930, when they released the cartoon "Mysterious Mose." The song used, "Mysterious Mose," had been written earlier that year by Walter Doyle and recorded by Ted Weems and his Orchestra. The song tells the story of a sly shape-changer roaming through the land. He often whistles and can appear anywhere at any time. According to the tune, "He sees all, he knows all, he gets in everywhere / Some night, he might wait for you upon the stair! / . . . / That's Mysterious Mose!"

Naturally, Bimbo played Mose. In the cartoon, Betty, who is alone in a huge old house, becomes so frightened, or excited, or both, at the sound of Bimbo-Mose's approach that her nightgown flies off her naked body twice as she sits trembling in bed, revealing part of her breasts each time.

Betty then reacts to Mose's actual appearance by swinging her hips back and forth toward him while still clad in her somewhat revealing nightgown. She also lofts Mose a small pillow shaped like a beating heart which she's liberated from her nightgown. As soon as the old house begins making strange creaking noises, however, Betty and Mose-Bimbo hug, but are too frightened to do anything else.

Apparently fearing that Betty's audience wouldn't like seeing two cartoons in a row that didn't imply that she was getting sex, even off-screen, the Fleischer brothers decided that their next Boop cartoon would go further. Fearful, however, that they'd look uncreative if they based more of their cartoons on recent popular songs, the brothers decided to base their next one, "Bum Bandit," released April 6, 1931, on a popular poem from 1907, "The Shooting of Dan McGrew," by Robert W. Service. According to the first stanza of that poem,

> *A bunch of the boys were whooping it up in the Malamute saloon.*
> *The kid that handles the music-box was hitting a jag-time tune*
> *Back of the bar, in a solo game, sat Dangerous Dan McGrew,*
> *And watching his luck was his light-o'-love, the lady that's known as Lou.*

Unfortunately for Lou and Dan, she kills him at the end of the poem, which had remained so popular for so many years that none other than Helen Kane had starred as "Nan McGrew" in the movie "Dangerous Nan McGrew," released in 1930. In that movie, Nan is a sharpshooter stranded in the Canadian northwest who puts on a show for a wealthy woman's Christmas Eve guests. The wealthy woman's nephew falls in love with Nan shortly before a bank robber crashes the party. The movie inspired the Fleischers to give Betty the same name, "Nan McGrew," in the "Bum Bandit" cartoon.

In that cartoon, Nan, played by Betty, is not only Dan's wife and the mother of the couple's seventeen children, she is also the engineer on a railroad train rolling through the western United States. When Dan the train robber, played by Bimbo, stops the train with the intention of robbing it, she immediately confronts him, denounces him for deserting her, and orders him to stop playing around and, by implication, to start playing with her once again.

A halfhearted bandit at best, Dan/Bimbo immediately complies with both requests, stealing no money or valuables while renewing his conjugal relationship with his wife. Although the actual sex is once again not shown, Mr. and Mrs. McGrew enter the engine cab, and a short while later their two sets of underwear are flying from a clothesline running from the engine's cab to its smokestack.

In any case, Betty's encounter with Bimbo in "Bum Bandit" seems not to have satisfied her. Only a few weeks later she is back in the city, taking a job as a singer in a variety show, as revealed in the cartoon "Silly Scandals," released May 23, 1931. In the cartoon, Bimbo comes to watch her perform. Probably to increase his interest in her, Betty allows the bodice of her dress to fall forward twice while she is singing, revealing her black bra each time. Bimbo is enchanted by Betty, who at this point still retains her cocker spaniel ears.

In the Betty Boop cartoon "Any Rags," released January 2, 1932, Bimbo, playing a rag man, sings the title song, composed by Thomas S. Allen and sung by Arthur Collins. This song was so old it was first recorded in 1903 on an Edison Cylinder, the first type of "record" ever produced, although the recording was later transferred to an actual flat vinyl record.

In the cartoon, apartment dweller Betty, hearing Bimbo's "Any Rags" rendition, alerts her neighbors and passersby to his presence by singing the traditional ditty "Stick Out Your Can, Here Comes the Garbage Man" from her third-floor window. (Although the name of its composer is unknown, "Stick Out Your Can" dated from the early 1900s.) Then, while informing Bimbo the Peddler from her third-floor apartment window that she doesn't have anything to give him, she manages to allow the top of her dress to fall down twice, again revealing her bra. As Betty intends, the provocative lyrics of "Stick Out Your Can" followed by the display of her partly nude upper body increase Bimbo's salacious interest in her shapely person. This display is especially notable because it is the first time that Betty appears on-screen with no canine features whatsoever.

Bimbo then takes Betty on an ice-skating date in the cartoon "Wait 'til the Sun Shines, Nellie," released on March 4, 1932. This cartoon was based on the song of the same name, written in 1905 by Harry Von Tilzer for his cousin Nellie Hyman. (Harry and Albert Von Tilzer were Jewish brothers and musicians who'd changed their last name from "Gumm" to sound more hip, a move the Fleischers hadn't bothered with.) Although the Fleischer brothers have Bimbo escort Betty on an ice-skating date in this cartoon, neither she nor Bimbo have enough energy left over for lovemaking after they've finished skating.

In "Let Me Call You Sweetheart," the accurately titled Betty-and-Bimbo cartoon released May 20, 1932, and based on the popular 1911 song of the same name, it becomes evident that Bimbo has become as sexually frustrated as Betty has been for months. When he meets her in a park, and sits down with her on a park bench, he grabs her by the shoulders and pulls her toward him. She falls across his lap looking sullen, but soon warms up to his newly aggressive approach. When darkness falls, the couple remain close together in the darkness with Bimbo's head on Betty's lap. It's unclear what happens when the camera isn't looking.

The musical portions of Betty's cartoons gave animators the opportunity to highlight some of the most important jazz performers in America. Unfortunately, along with this came some of the most racially offensive segments they ever created.

In the 1930s, racial segregation ruled in every aspect of American life. It was enforced by law in the South and by custom in the North. And, except as criminal suspects, convicts, or objects of ridicule, Black Americans rarely appeared in any form of the white media, including animated cartoons or comic strips. It wasn't until 1934, after Betty's career began, that the first Black comic strip character, Lothar, showed up in a strip titled "Mandrake the Magician." Lothar, a circus strongman, was Mandrake's sidekick. Poor and uneducated, he wore a Tarzan-style costume. In general, from then on Black people in comic strips were usually depicted as comic foils, low-level manual laborers, servants, ignorant natives, brutal savages, or cannibals.

Black characters were more prevalent in animated cartoons but weren't treated much better on-screen than they were on the page. No cartoon producers prior to the Fleischers had created characters based on real African Americans.

Some Black popular musicians, however, including the Mills Brothers, had appeared in the Fleischers' "Song Car-Tunes," the animations that used an illustrated bouncing ball to encourage audiences to sing along with filmed human singers. And because the Harlem Renaissance was underway, Max, Dave, and Lou Fleischer, and many of their employees, often visited Harlem's Black clubs, becoming enthusiastic fans of jazz.

As author Nathan Irvin Huggins noted, Harlem's Cotton Club and its competitors were "decorated with tropical and jungle motifs—some of them replicas of southern plantations." At these clubs, the audiences would hear jazz, which at that time was considered not only exotic, but in the words of one fan, "instinctive and abandoned . . . melody skipping atop inexorable driving rhythm." The fan added that, "in the darkness and closeness, the music, infectious and unrelenting, drove on."

Inspired by the Harlem scene, the Fleischers included film and/or animated versions of three major Black musicians and their orchestras in five of Betty's best cartoons. The musicians included Cab Calloway in the cartoons "Minnie the Moocher," "Snow-White," and "The Old Man of the Mountain"; Louis Armstrong in "I'll Be Glad When You're Dead, You Rascal You"; and Don Redman in "I Heard." By screening films and cartoons of these Black musicians and bands in performance, the Fleischers were anticipating the founding of the cable channel Music Television (MTV) by forty-nine years.

They also were years ahead of MTV in another way. Even though much of America was strictly segregated during the first three decades of Betty's career, most of the musicians employed on screen in her cartoons were nonwhite. By contrast, for several years after MTV was founded in 1981, it refused to broadcast videos produced by prominent African American singers and musicians.

Later critics have argued that there were some downsides to the Fleischers' portrayals of Black musicians. All three of Betty's cartoons featuring Cab Calloway show Betty being pursued or frightened by monsters (although the monsters themselves are not always Black). Author Jake Austen has contended that this illustrated an underlying fear of Black people. Also, in the cartoon "I'll Be Glad When You're Dead, You Rascal You," the Fleischers racially mocked Louis Armstrong, his drummer, and, by implication, all the other members of his band, and all Black people.

In spite of these interpretations, the musicians involved welcomed the Fleischers' attentions, partly because each cartoon started off with a filmed performance by the vocalist or orchestra leader and his ensemble before the cartoon itself began. The musicians appreciated the fact that showing these cartoons resulted in profitable publicity for the bands involved.

They were particularly grateful that the Fleischers and Paramount Pictures Corporation, the Fleischers' financier and distributor, coordinated the release of the cartoons with the musicians' in-person appearances in cities where the cartoons were being shown, thus increasing ticket sales for the musicians' performances. The effect on ticket sales was quite significant, partly because Betty's cartoons were so popular that they were sometimes billed above feature films on theater marquees. Under normal circumstances, renting an equipped studio in which to film the musicians performing for the filmed portion of each cartoon would have been beyond the Fleischers' budget. Paramount, however, allowed the Fleischers to use its newsreel filming facilities for this purpose at no charge.

Betty's partnership with famous Black musicians got off to a great start with the release of her cartoon "Minnie the Moocher" on February 26, 1932. The song of the same name had been recorded by Cab

Calloway in 1931 and had gone on to sell over a million copies worldwide. The words to the song are often nonsensical and indecipherable, partly because Calloway loved singing improvised nonsense syllables in place of the lyrics—a technique known as scat singing—and partly because the "Minnie" song originated in the 1927 tune "Willie the Weeper" by Frankie "Half Pint" Jaxon. Jaxon loved street slang and often referred obliquely to drugs in his compositions. To create the "Minnie the Moocher" song, Calloway creatively combined "Willie the Weeper" with a song titled "Minnie the Mermaid" that had been written by B. G. De Sylva.

Calloway appears in a filmed segment at the start of the cartoon, the earliest known film of him and his ten-piece orchestra. His swaying, strutting, pirouetting style was so unique that the Fleischers rotoscoped his movements so they could be used by characters who were portraying him in the cartoon section of the film. While arranging this, the Fleischers had no way of knowing that in both the film segment and

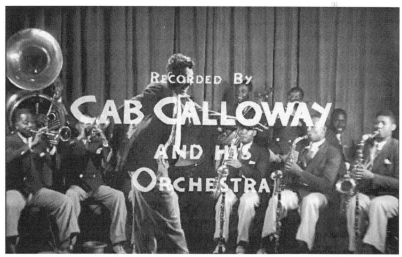

The Cab Calloway segment that opened "Minnie the Moocher" (1932) is the earliest known film of him and his jazz orchestra.

the cartoon itself, Calloway would be performing a step that anticipated Michael Jackson's moonwalk some twenty-five years before Jackson was born.

Although the film is named after the song "Minnie the Moocher,"
the tune Calloway dances to in his filmed performance at the beginning of the cartoon while backed by his orchestra is the introductory
section to the song "St. James Infirmary Blues," not the introduction to "Minnie the Moocher," the cartoon's title song. The same
procedure was followed in the four other cartoons in which Betty
interacted with Black musicians: the musical piece after which the
cartoon was named was played only after the cartoon section of the
film began, instead of in the introductory section, in which each band
played on camera.

Author Daniel Goldmark has argued that this technique was aimed
at keeping viewers' attention on the cartoon's characters, instead of on
the song and the musicians playing it. This is unlike, say, modern music
videos, in which a band plays its own popular song throughout the
video and all the viewers' attention throughout the film is focused on
the band members themselves.

The cartoon portion of "Minnie the Moocher" begins when Betty,
angry at being urged to overeat by her parents, runs away from home
with her dog Bimbo, and hides with him in a nearby cave. (One notable feature of this cartoon is that although Betty calls Bimbo on the
phone to arrange their plan to run away, when the two of them return
home at the end of the cartoon Bimbo takes shelter in his kennel,
which is right outside Betty's house. Had Mr. and Mrs. Boop installed
a telephone in their daughter's dog's kennel?) Betty and Bimbo quickly
arrive at the cave. Caves appear in all three Betty Boop cartoons in

which Calloway participated, leading some critics to argue that by consistently using a cave for its performance, the Fleischers were using yet another technique to label Calloway's music, and perhaps all Black music, as scary.

In this perhaps controversial setting, Calloway materializes as a ghostly walrus and sings the "Minnie the Moocher" song, accompanied by his now-invisible orchestra. He also dances and struts in front of an ever-changing cave wall of bizarre images. The walrus version, based on a rotoscope of the musician, dances exactly like Calloway. (Author Jake Austen contends that although the walrus version of Calloway is gray and white, rather than black, the walrus's long tail represents a long waggling penis, in line with a stereotype about Black men.)

Calloway also appears in "Minnie the Moocher" as a ghostly walrus.

In any case, Calloway certainly seems to be referencing Black people in the song. Among the verses that Calloway the walrus sings in the cave is one about how Minnie, "a red hot hoochie coocher," or belly dancer, "messed around with a bloke named Smokey," and loved him "though he was cokey." Many viewers may have failed to realize that Calloway was calling Smokey a cocaine addict, and that judging by his nickname, he was probably a Black man. Calloway went on to reveal in song that Smokey then took Minnie to Chinatown, where they "kicked the gong around," meaning that they scored some heroin.

As Calloway the walrus continues to perform in the cartoon, the cave wall behind him comes alive with surrealistically portrayed humans and animals that scare poor Bimbo and Betty nearly to death. Among them are ghostly convicts dancing in and out of their cells before being executed by an equally ghostly electrocutioner, beer-drinking skeletons, and a scat-singing momma cat with her scat-singing kittens. Nursing on their mother, the kittens empty her of milk, doubling their own size and weight as she shrinks to near nothingness.

While Calloway keeps on singing and dancing in the foreground, Bimbo and Betty continue to watch nervously until a genuinely frightening witch flies directly at them and the viewer. The witch's wide-open mouth, which displays only one tooth and fills the entire screen, comes so close to the viewer that the screen is dominated by the two, fleshy, worm-like uvulae at the back of her mouth. The witch's uncanny screeching fills everyone's ears.

These sights and sounds may have caused many children, and a few nervous adults, to run screaming out of theaters where "Minnie the Moocher" was playing. The ruckus certainly is scary enough to chase the already trembling and shaken Bimbo and Betty out of the cave. They are vigorously pursued by a shrieking ghostly horde to the strains of "Tiger Rag," also known as "Hold That Tiger," an immensely popular song first recorded by the all-white band known as the Original Dixieland Jass Band in 1917 and played by Calloway's orchestra in the cartoon.

Despite some of the criticisms aimed at the "Minnie the Moocher" cartoon, Dave Fleischer claimed that when Calloway saw the finished film, he "laughed so much that he fell right down on the floor of the projection room and kicked his feet in the air." Whether this actually happened is uncertain; Calloway looks like a very neat and composed fellow. But he certainly seemed to like the cartoon. Some forty-four years later, in fact, he raved about the song in his autobiography, *Of Minnie the Moocher & Me*. Calloway wrote that the song "shows that it's possible to follow your dreams and to live the way you want to live and to be free with your emotions and to express what you feel deeply." Betty couldn't have said it better. The "Minnie the Moocher" cartoon went on to enjoy a revival as a "head film" for marijuana and narcotics users in the 1960s.

Another film in which Calloway appeared was "Snow-White," which was released on March 1, 1933. Calloway's performance is partly a repeat of his "Minnie the Moocher" performance. This time disguised as Koko the Clown rather than a walrus, Calloway performs the first half of the "St. James Infirmary" song about halfway into the film, as he follows Snow-White's coffin. This makes perfect sense, since the song describes going "to see my baby's coffin at the infirmary." About halfway through the song, however, the wicked witch uses her magic mirror to transform Calloway into a flexible, long-legged, short-jacketed ghost. In this guise he does a magnificent job of singing the tune's second half.

Calloway's final contribution to Betty's opus occurred when he allowed his 1932 performance of the song "The Old Man of the Mountain," written by white songwriters Billy Hill and Victor Young, to be used as the basis of Betty's cartoon of the same name, released on August 4, 1933. The cartoon begins with a live film of Calloway and his orchestra performing the "Hi-de-ho" section of "Minnie the Moocher." As the "Old Man" cartoon begins, Betty, apparently hoping that a change of scene and some vigorous outdoor exercise will do her some good, takes a train to a hilly rural area miles from her home. She then starts walking along a trail up the mountain that dominates the region.

On the way, Betty talks with some locals who tell her that the area's best-known resident, an older fellow, is nicknamed "The Old Man of the Mountain." They describe him as having "a long white beard and a crooked step" and claim that women move aside in fright as he tramps along, because he passes them by with a lecherous "twinkle in his eye." All of these are taken from lines in the song "The Old Man of the Mountain." The locals warn her to stay away from the old man, but Betty, wearing her usual short skirt and garter even while hiking, tells them she wants to meet him.

She continues to search for the Old Man even after passing an overweight woman, portrayed in the cartoon as having a face that resembles a hippo's. The woman is wheeling a stroller occupied by triplets, all of whom are obviously the old man's progeny: they all look like him, beards and all. Far from rejoicing in motherhood, the woman weeps copiously about her plight and warns Betty to avoid the Old Man. But this only spurs Betty on.

When she encounters The Old Man himself, he is obviously pleased and astonished to see her mincing, hip-shaking, underdressed, conspicuously

The titular character advances on Betty in "The Old Man of the Mountain" (1933).

urban self in such a rural setting. But Betty, after actually meeting him, is momentarily shocked at his appearance: he is old, ugly, and wearing an animal skin, with his huge tongue hanging out of his mouth.

Nevertheless, when the Old Man strokes her chin with his beard, Betty finds herself unable to entirely break old habits. She playfully pulls on the man's beard, causing him to come on to her again. Being younger and faster, however, Betty manages to escape him and return safely to the city.

Some critics have argued that "The Old Man of the Mountain," cartoon has racist overtones. There are viewers who believe the Old Man appears to be Black, and author Austen has also noted that later in the cartoon, when the Old Man is finally subdued, his phallic nose is long enough to be tied in a knot and hung flaccidly, allegedly another nod to racist stereotypes about Black men's genitals. Others have pointed out that while the Old Man's skin is somewhat darker than Betty's, it could easily be attributed to his spending most of his days outdoors. And the Old Man's use of Calloway's voice is obviously connected to the fact that Calloway sang the song in its most popular version. The fact that the Old Man's nose is so long it could be tied in a knot is certainly not supported by earlier depictions of his nose in the cartoon, and in any case, it's more believable as simply a nonracist absurdism.

For the most part, in four of the five Fleischer cartoons highlighting Black musicians, those musicians are treated respectfully. The exception was Louis Armstrong, who appeared in only one Fleischer cartoon, "I'll Be Glad When You're Dead You Rascal You," which was released on November 25, 1932. In this cartoon, Armstrong and his nine-man, all-Black orchestra appeared in person and in animated form and were treated shamefully.

Named after the song of the same name written by African American composer Sam Theard, the cartoon, a racist classic, opens with film of Armstrong and his orchestra performing the tune "High Society," a 1901 jazz standard written by Porter Steele. (Steele, a white man whose father was attorney general of Louisiana, was undoubtedly acquainted with high society.) As the cartoon begins with Bimbo and Koko carrying white hunter Betty Boop through the African jungle on a litter, Armstrong and his band play the "I'll Be Glad" tune off-screen. Betty, nicely tanned, is sitting upright wearing a blouse, skirt, and pith helmet. The litter bounces considerably while it's being carried, allowing the animators to pointedly highlight Betty's body.

The three travelers are soon observed by some stereotypical African tribesmen wearing large earrings and banana-leaf skirts. Some of them

The disembodied head of Louis Armstrong pursues Koko the Clown in "I'll Be Glad When You're Dead You Rascal You" (1932).

carry a fork in one hand and a knife in the other: obviously, they're cannibals. A mob of them kidnaps Betty, leaving Bimbo, Koko, and the now-destroyed litter sitting on the road.

Outraged, Koko starts referring to the cannibals as "babies," invoking the racist term "Jungle Babies" that was common at the time. Bimbo and Koko then track the tribesmen to their village, where the cannibals are dancing around a large cooking pot. The tribesmen immediately spot the pair and throw them into the pot. Our two heroes soon escape and have just begun running away when a huge cartoon head of Armstrong sporting exaggeratedly thick white lips and a cannibal hairdo appears above them. As Armstrong sings the song "I'll Be Glad When You're Dead You Rascal You," our terrified heroes increase their speed. Shortly thereafter, Armstrong's cartoon cannibal head morphs into his actual head once again before a film of Armstrong and his band playing the rest of the song appears on the screen.

(The audience for the cartoon section of this production may have found it confusing that while Armstrong keeps singing at this point, it soon becomes apparent that the lyrics of his song don't always mesh with what's happening in the cartoon. For instance, he appears to be singing about another man flirting with or having sex with his wife in such verses as "I brought you into my home, you won't leave my wife alone," and "What is it that you've got, that makes my wife think you're hot?" Mrs. Armstrong does not appear at all in the film, however, and the cartoon fails to explain this discrepancy.)

As Armstrong goes on to sing the questionable line, "You bought my wife a bottle of Coca-Cola so you could play on her Victrola," his filmed face becomes that of the cartoon cannibal once again. And a couple of seconds later, a cartoon image of him dressed and acting like a cannibal and carrying a spear appears in the cartoon itself. Armstrong hurls a spear at Koko but misses.

A club-wielding Bimbo soon appears behind Armstrong, clubs him, and throws him in a trash can. Bimbo and Koko then complete their escape as the real Armstrong and his orchestra appear on the screen playing the song "Chinatown," a jazz standard.

Bimbo and Koko soon return to the village to rescue Betty, who's now tied tightly to a stake as the cartoon cannibals dance around her and menace her with their knives and forks. One cannibal, presumably reacting to Betty's exposed cleavage, tries to kiss her, but she pulls on his nose ring to discourage him. As she continues to struggle to free herself from the stake, however, she ends up wriggling alluringly. While Betty is being slowly roasted, the camera focuses on an overweight female cannibal who is moving her head back and forth while pounding two cooking implements up and down in the cooking pot. Unforgivably, the camera then shifts to a film of the overweight male drummer in Armstrong's band, Albert "Tubby" Hall, making similar movements with his head and one of his drumsticks.

Back in the cartoon, Bimbo and Koko rescue Betty, and as they flee, Betty's sexpot nature is emphasized: while the cannibals throw spears at her, she jumps up and down and squeals each time one of these long jungle sticks comes close. The enraged cannibals chase the trio to the top of a volcano and our heroes start their downhill run just before it explodes, blowing their pursuers into the sky. The camera immediately cuts to Armstrong and band playing the peroration of the song, in which Armstrong sings its last line, "I'll be glad when you're dead, you rascal you," seeming to refer to the now presumably dead cannibals. (In the song itself, Armstrong is referring to the man who seduced his wife.)

Although entertaining, this cartoon presents a Black twentieth-century American orchestra leader and his drummer as cannibals solely on the basis of their skin color. Armstrong's thoughts about the cartoon went unrecorded, but it's unlikely that he laughed hysterically while watching this racist production unfold.

Armstrong did issue a comment of sorts while the film/cartoon was still being prepared. As he and his band were being filmed playing the "I'll Be Glad When You're Dead" song, he kept dancing out of camera range as if he wanted to leave the production entirely. The producers were finally forced to draw a chalk mark on the floor and tell him to stay near it. The only way he could force himself to do that, however, was to look down at the mark and comment on it.

So as filming resumed, Armstrong kept looking down and singing "'I'll be glad when you're dead, you rascal you.' Where's that line?" At least he was trying to stay on the correct side of the line; the writers and animators of the film took no such precautions.

There's no indication that anyone criticized the cartoon when it appeared. Even if someone had done so, criticism of this sort didn't appear to faze the Fleischers all that much.

5

THE SURREAL STYLE

By 1931, the Fleischers had spent most of their Betty-related energy so far on animating her to be as sexy as possible and spend most of her time seeking and finding a male love interest. At this point, however, they were also starting to explore more innovative visual and storytelling techniques, particularly surrealistic ones.

Cartoons and surrealism were a perfect match, because even in non-surrealistic cartoons, reality is distorted and stretched. As Dave Fleischer often told his artists, "If it can be done in real life, it isn't animation." What this meant in practice was that even the earliest Fleischer cartoons became partly surreal as various inanimate objects in those cartoons developed lips and eyes. It's true that many of Betty's cartoons were little more than sequences of sight gags set to music. Some of Betty's most remarkable cartoons, however, start out somewhat conventionally but almost immediately rocket toward total surrealism.

Among these cartoons were "Bimbo's Initiation," released on July 27, 1931, which featured multiple clones of Betty trying to convince Bimbo to join their literally underground society; "Minnie the Moocher," released on February 26, 1932, which begins with Betty running away from home when her parents insist that she clean her plate; and "Snow-White," released on March 1, 1933. (The "Snow-White" cartoon's creative surrealism caused the National Film Registry to select it for historic preservation in 1996. It shouldn't be confused, however, with Walt Disney's *Snow White and the Seven Dwarfs*. That cartoon was released five years later, although both versions were based on the fairy tale first published by the Brothers Grimm in 1812.)

What made the Fleischers' surrealistic cartoons different from their other releases was that they relied on a series of bizarre, constantly changing images. Both the people and the animals in these cartoons often appeared, disappeared, flew away, changed shape, or changed into other people, plants, or animals, thus resembling beings often encountered in dreams or nightmares. The Fleischer cartoons that

Clones of Betty trying to lure Bimbo in "Bimbo's Initiation" (1931).

The Fleischers' "Snow-White" (1933) was considerably stranger than Disney's version of the story. PHOTOFEST.

featured these images could also be identified by their jazz soundtracks and spooky backgrounds.

Although the Fleischers were among the pioneers in the use of surrealism in cartoons, in 1910 one of the world's first animators, the Frenchman Emile Cohl, produced cartoons in which houses turned into huge heads and trees became people. When the Fleischers and their animators had Betty act in surrealistic cartoons, however, they were reacting not to Cohl but to the rise of non-animated surrealist movies. Although such films were partly realistic, they drew much of their inspiration from Freudian dream imagery and the imaginings of the subconscious mind that Freud had popularized in his books and lectures on the subject.

Surrealism had also influenced several painters, including Salvador Dalí. His best-known paintings include images of gigantic melting pocket watches and walls that go nowhere and shield nothing. *Un Chien Andalou* ("An Andalusian Dog"), a surrealist film that Dalí and Luis Buñuel produced in 1929, included a scene of a woman's eyeball being cut vertically with a razor blade for no rational reason. This and several other aspects of that movie startled the film world and influenced many producers and directors, including Max Fleischer. He was particularly attracted to *The Cabinet of Dr. Caligari*, a 1930 surrealist film. In that movie, shadows and streaks of light are painted directly onto the movie's sets rather than appearing naturally, and the buildings themselves lean and twist at unusual angles. Some of the characters influence each other by projecting their thoughts directly into the minds of others.

When Max Fleischer's son Richard was about seven, he and his father attended a daytime showing of this film in an art house theater in Manhattan. "I never forgot the experience," Richard wrote years later. "I still carry an image from it around in my head—a tall, pale-faced thin man in a long black coat, his eyes circled in black, standing in a narrow hallway, its walls askew. I remember not so much being frightened as somehow being hypnotized by the image."

(Richard Fleischer later became a film director. Although none of the films he directed were surrealistic, many of them were highly praised and very popular. They included *20,000 Leagues Under the Sea* [1954], *The Vikings* [1958], *Compulsion* [1959], *The Boston Strangler* [1968], *Tora! Tora! Tora!* [1970], *Soylent Green* [1973], *Mandingo* [1975], *Conan the Destroyer* [1984], and *Red Sonja* [1985].)

Richard's father, Max, was so impressed by *The Cabinet of Dr. Caligari* that he extended its influence into several Betty Boop cartoons. As a result, Betty's surrealistic cartoons were somewhat quirky and dark, and lightened only slightly by her considerable charm.

Surrealism, coupled with German Expressionism (which Betty's creator, Grim Natwick, had studied for two years in Germany before signing on with the Fleischers), dominated the cartoon titled "Bimbo's Initiation." It was released on July 27, 1931, with Betty playing a significant role. This cartoon slowly reveals that Betty had been tasked with offering her erotic services to a secret society that was trying to attract Bimbo as a member. A plot problem linked to this cartoon immediately confronted the Fleischers, however. Why would Bimbo, a normal dog-man, want to be a member of a weird-looking society that met beneath street level? Dogs and dog/men traditionally favored open air, streets, and parks, as Bimbo had done in most of his other Fleischer films.

A solution soon presented itself to Max and Dave, however. They already were having nightmares over the stiff competition they were facing from California's Walt Disney Studios. Swept up by paranoia, or reacting to the reality of big-time competition, they began to think that Disney would be very pleased to weaken them by pushing one of their major characters, Bimbo, in front of a bus, throwing him off a cliff, or locking him into an underground world where he'd be trapped forever.

And to whom would Disney entrust to such a sensitive task? Obviously, to his major character and own personal invention, his chef d'oeuvre, none other than Mickey Mouse. Therefore, the Fleischers arranged for the "Bimbo's Initiation" cartoon to begin with Bimbo walking down the street and accidentally falling into an open man-hole. Numerous such accidents occur every year, but something special occurs in this cartoon as soon as Bimbo disappears: a character resembling Mickey Mouse races onto the scene and clicks a padlock onto the now-closed manhole cover. Mickey's obvious intention: to make certain that Bimbo will never ever appear aboveground again to threaten Disney's hoped-for dominance of cartoon world.

The rest of "Bimbo's Initiation" unfolds like a bad dream in which Bimbo, trapped in an underground maze, is pursued by bouncing, hooded figures who force him into one harrowing predicament after another. Each figure is wearing a burned-down candle on his head and carrying a spiked two-by-four behind his back. The figures keep pushing Bimbo deeper into a nightmarish world from which he cannot escape. He hears them continually asking, "Wanna be a member? Wanna be a member?" A request he refuses many times.

Bimbo's refusals result in many new horrors: an immense knife licking its chops, a room turned upside down, a door that looks like a way out but leads only to more dangers, and a bicycle that sets fire to anyone who rides it. To top this all off, when he tries to escape, he finds himself running backward rather than forward.

Bimbo's torture continues until Betty appears and tells him to "Come inside, Big Boy," an obvious sexual invitation. Bimbo follows Betty down a long, unmistakably vaginal corridor in which huge blades slash savagely downward, barely missing him and seemingly threatening him with castration.

As soon as Bimbo arrives at the end of the corridor, Betty appears, performs an erotic dance in front of him, and asks, "Wanna be a member?" (The use of the word "member" in such a sexual context was obviously one of the Fleischers' little jokes.) Bimbo, being no fool, this time says yes. A few seconds later, he finds himself surrounded by either multiple Betty Boops or clones of her, all dancing and singing to celebrate his accession to membership.

Bimbo confronts assorted surreal horrors in "Bimbo's Initiation" (1931).

Author Leslie Cabarga notes that this cartoon might as well be a catalog of the occult for all the symbolism it employs. Many people who saw it probably experienced the same disorientation and wonder that *The Cabinet of Dr. Caligari* invoked in Richard Fleischer.

"Bimbo's Initiation" also illustrates the Freudian observation that the conscious and the unconscious often interact. In many scenes, much of the action occurs directly in front of the audience, but various background figures and objects simultaneously act out their own dramas and compulsions. The action on both levels becomes so entwined that the background and the foreground, like the conscious and unconscious mind, feed into each other. As a result, viewers react to films like these with both their conscious and unconscious selves, doubling their impact.

Author Stefan Kanfer makes the additional claim that "Bimbo's Initiation" should be classified as a precursor of the film noir movement.

Noir films also feature stark backgrounds and take place in a world dominated by insecurity and dread.

Although this cartoon was the high point of the Fleischers' infatuation with surrealism and stunned many of Betty's fans, the brothers kept playing around with surrealism in their later cartoons. On January 27, 1933, for instance, the Fleischers released "Betty Boop's Crazy Inventions," in which a runaway sewing machine begins by stitching people together and sewing their mouths shut. It then closes up ditches while they're being dug, sews riverbanks together, and finally stitches up the entire world. Surrealism had finally—and completely—triumphed.

More broadly, dreams—and the surreal logic that so often shape them—were a frequent feature of Betty's cartoons. They were often characterized by romantic conflict. In the cartoon "Chess Nuts," released on April 19, 1932, Betty dreams she is a piece in a chess game. (The game had become increasingly popular among American women in the 1930s; the first women's chess championship in the United States was held in 1937, and the US Chess Federation was founded in 1939.) Specifically, Betty is the black queen in a chess game being played on a football-sized field by a mixed group of humans and animals, including Bimbo. In Betty's dream she is married to the black king— an unattractive, dirty old white man—while Bimbo plays the White King. The conflict in Betty's mind between what she most wants—to be with Bimbo—and what society says she must do—remain faithful to her husband—is demonstrated throughout the cartoon. When her husband wants to tie her to a chair, with all of the sexual over tones that entails, Betty responds somewhat enticingly: "Hello, Kingy! Hello, Kingy!" Only when the king actually gropes her while standing

Betty and the black king in "Chess Nuts" (1932).

behind her does Betty say, "Oh no!" She then assumes a boxer's stance and begins fighting him until he picks her up and ties her to a pillar. Betty continues to express her conflicted thoughts by repeating her enticement of "Hello, Kingy!" Obviously, she can't bring herself to completely reject her own husband. Only once Bimbo has finally defeated the black king with his doggy fists and rescued Betty does she awake from her strange dream.

Only ten days later, on April 29, the cartoon "A-Hunting We Will Go" was released. In this cartoon Betty has rented a cabin and placed a sign over her bed reading "Nuts." (In this instance, the Fleischers were forfeiting all claims to subtlety.) We see and hear Betty playing the piano in the cabin while singing a song that begins "I want to have a fur coat, have a fur coat, not until then will I be happy . . . I want to find that man, I'd love him a lot. If I could find that man, I'd give him all that I've got."

Bimbo and Koko, two dedicated urbanites and male friends of Betty's who are hunting nearby, hear her singing and come rushing in. They stroke her bare arms and legs, telling her, "OK, baby, we'll take you out." Both soon realize that the Fleischers aren't going to let them spend the night with Betty without a significant investment, so they leave the cabin to go hunting for furs for her coat. After numerous adventures, they come back a few days later with an enormous pile of furs to show her. Betty, however, takes note of the group of naked, furless animals that have followed Bimbo and Koko back to the cabin. She rejects both of them, and becomes the heroine of a local animal parade, wearing a magnificent fur coat as she marches.

Almost two years later, Betty is shown once again living in a big old house in the city and seemingly very desirous of companionship. As documented in the cartoon "Red Hot Mamma," released on February 2, 1934, Betty is sleeping at home alone when the temperature drops. Awakened by the cold, she throws some logs on the fire and falls back asleep. She awakens in dreamland, which in this cartoon is a steaming hot hellscape. Wearing only her nightgown, she begins exploring her new environment. Soon, the dreaming, underclad Betty comes across a group of black devils attaching tails to young white devils who live in a building labeled "Freshman Hall." Apparently aroused by the implicitly sexual activity, she immediately starts singing a song: "Hells Bells ringing in my ear make me hot."

Several of the black devils in Betty's dream, attracted by her singing, surround her and begin to approach her. But Betty, who can be cold when she really wants to be, literally ices them with a chilly stare and

Betty's fireplace is a gateway to a bizarre hellscape in "Red Hot Mamma" (1934).

wakes up at home, safe in her bed. Betty, although seemingly tempted by sex, has subconsciously rejected it—perhaps condemning herself to years of sexual disappointment, or perhaps realizing for the first time that there are other things more important to her.

6

THE HAYS OFFICE
LOWERS THE BOOM

Betty Boop was undoubtedly the world's first mainstream animated sex symbol. And as time went on, her behavior in cartoons became more and more liberated and her outfits skimpy and tight fitting. This was at a time when sexual content and partial nudity were becoming more common in Hollywood films. Movies that featured scantily clad actresses and bloodsucking monsters attracted large crowds of viewers eager for distraction from the misery of the Great Depression. *The Barbarian* featured a married couple who enjoyed slapping and whipping each other. *The Aviator*, a Howard Hughes film, featured open-mouthed kissing in which British soldiers and French barmaids appeared to be trying to swallow each other, according to one shocked reviewer. Women in films could often be seen slinging one leg over the arm of a chair while swinging the other leg back and forth and otherwise being sexually assertive. Archetypes of the "fallen woman," "possessed woman," and "kept woman" dominated the silver screen during these years. Viewers were unlikely to complain about Betty's relationship with Bimbo after Paramount released the horror film *Dr. Jekyll and Mr. Hyde*. The critics who viewed that movie called it "raw, brutal and relentlessly sexual," and wrote that the love scenes between actors Frederic March and Miriam Hopkins "smacked of bestiality." And no holds were barred in MGM's jungle movies, in which seminude natives and explorers were routinely whipped and tortured.

Betty continued her sex romp in "Stopping the Show," released on August 12, 1932. In this cartoon, she imitates other celebrities, such as Fanny Brice and Maurice Chevalier, on stage. While changing from female to male attire on stage as she prepares to imitate Chevalier, Betty manages once again to reveal her bra to the mostly male audience, which rewards her with such a resounding ovation that the next act on the bill is unable to begin.

So no one could blame Betty when she took a vacation on a South Pacific Island in the cartoon "Betty Boop's Bamboo Isle," released on September 23, 1932. The cartoon begins with a lively filmed performance by the real-life band the Royal Samoans featuring the female dancer Lotamuru, who performs an energetic hula backed by nine bare-chested men wearing leis and lava-lavas who pick and strum guitars, pound drums, shake rattles, and clap their hands to the pulsating hula rhythms. In the animated segment, Bimbo, after locating Betty on the island, is pleasantly surprised to see that she's acquired a magnificent tan and is dancing on the beach wearing only a grass skirt and a lei.

Betty continued this theme in "Is My Palm Read?" a suggestively titled cartoon that the Fleischers released on February 17, 1933. Appropriately enough, Betty appears in the cartoon wearing a diaphanous skirt, a stylish blouse, and a wide-brimmed hat to visit a fortune-telling

A scantily clad, pre-Code Betty in "Betty Boop's Bamboo Isle" (1932).

parlor that Bimbo and Koko have recently opened. At one point, as a flutist begins playing behind her, she shimmies in her revealing outfit, delighting the two "swamis." And in "Poor Cinderella," released on August 3, 1934—the first, and only, color cartoon the Fleischers created for Betty—a fairy godmother uses her magic wand to strip Betty of her worn and patched outer clothing, revealing her bra and slip.

The Fleischers and their animators almost always directed Betty to react with grace and humor to advances by various male admirers. At the same time, a recurring element in their cartoons around this time was men embarrassing themselves sexually with inappropriately timed erections—unsurprising given the youth and relative inexperience of many of Betty's creators. At one point in "Betty Boop's Bamboo Isle," when Betty is doing a hula on the beach wearing a grass skirt with only a lei barely covering her breasts, Bimbo becomes so excited watching her that he's forced to snatch a pair of grass shorts to better cover his own pelvis, which then begins undulating vigorously back and forth in Betty's direction. (Betty also looks embarrassed and covers her eyes.)

In a later cartoon, Betty embarrasses her fellow Fleischer character Popeye under very similar circumstances. This was, in fact, the very first Popeye cartoon, "Popeye the Sailor," released on July 14, 1933. Apparently inspired by Betty's hula dancing and Bimbo's reaction to it in their "Betty Boop's Bamboo Isle," cartoon, the Fleischers had Betty perform a similar dance onstage at a carnival on the US mainland for Popeye and others in the crowd. Betty's alluring dance attracts Popeye's attention to such an extent that he hops up on stage and becomes so excited that he grabs the fake facial hair from Madame Hari, a bearded lady, to cover his lower half.

Of course, sex was not the only "sinful" topic depicted in Betty's cartoons. Alcohol was also celebrated in a number of them: when she becomes president of the United States in her "Betty Boop for President" cartoon, released on November 4, 1932, she repeals Prohibition.

Betty reprised her hula dance in "Popeye the Sailor" (1933).

And in Betty's 1933 cartoon "The Old Man of the Mountain," two fleas living in the old man's beard pour a mug of beer down his throat as he chases Betty.

The Fleischers even allowed her to do drugs on one occasion, as documented in Betty's cartoon "Ha! Ha! Ha!" released on March 2, 1934. In this cartoon, Betty has taken a new job as a receptionist in a dentist's office when her old pal, Koko, tells her he is suffering from a toothache but can't afford a dentist. So, after the dentist has left, Betty tries unsuccessfully to remove his aching tooth with a pair of pliers. Her strenuous efforts to extract it, however, cause her old friend terrible pain, so she administers laughing gas, which sends him into uncontrolled paroxysms of laughter. When Betty accidentally breathes some in herself, she joins Koko in his laughing fit, after which the gas then billows out the window onto what appears to be a Manhattan street, causing crowds of nearby pedestrians to break into convulsive laughter. The pedestrians appear in a filmed rather than an animated portion of the cartoon, with their laughter dubbed onto the soundtrack.

(Although the Fleischers may not have realized it, Betty's use of laughing gas was a throwback to nineteenth-century Britain, when members of the upper class, on learning how intoxicating nitrous oxide could be, held laughing gas parties at each other's homes at which they all breathed in the gas, laughed hysterically, and felt *great!*)

The content of Betty's cartoons did not go unnoticed by organizations such as the National Legion of Decency, whose officials argued that her neckline was too low, her dress was too short, and both her garter and her walk were too suggestive and incited sexual arousal. In 1933, even a theater owner who was presumably making money on Betty's displays went so far as to write a letter to the *Film Daily*, a newspaper that covered the entertainment industry, complaining that there was too much smut in cartoons.

Betty was merely keeping in step with the rest of the film industry, however. Many female movie stars besides her were shedding more and more clothes, and more and more scruples, on-screen. In fact, many live performers went even further than Betty did. In the movie *Girls About Town*, released in 1931, actress Kay Francis played an attractive young "escort" named Wanda who accepts extravagant gifts for going out on "dates" with middle-aged men; at one point, Wanda tells a girl-friend that "I've got a callus on my knee from my boyfriend's subtle approach." In the movie *Red-Headed Woman*, released in 1932, actress Jean Harlow played Lil "Red" Andrews, who is stalking William "Bill" Legendre, played by Chester Morris. When Legendre visits Lil's apartment to tell her to leave him alone, she locks the door from the inside, and, after a couple of minutes of arguing, an either enraged or aroused Bill slaps Lil hard across her face, to which she responds, panting, "Do it again. I like it!"

Mae West was also way ahead of Betty. West had first come to public attention when she starred in a 1926 Broadway play unambiguously titled *Sex*, which resulted in a ten-day jail term for her for "corrupting the morals of youth." She was hardly subdued by her time behind bars, however. In the 1930s, following her film debut in *Night after Night* starring George Raft, West became, according to one wag, "As hot an issue as Hitler." West was even memorialized in the title of one of Betty's cartoons, "She Wronged Him Right," a take-off on the title of West's movie *She Done Him Wrong*.

In 1930, the Motion Picture Producers and Distributors of America (MPPDA) had enacted the Hays Code, which was aimed at the writers and producers of movies and cartoons. Will Hays was an elder in the Presbyterian Church, as well as a former postmaster general under President Warren G. Harding, and the former head of the Republican National Committee. Day-to-day censorship, however, was carried out by his employee Joseph Breen, who was hired to administer the code in Hollywood.

Although the code had been adopted in 1930, enforcement of it did not really begin until 1934. The regulations included a rule stating that "No picture shall be produced that will lower the moral standards of those who see it." Other relevant provisions included:

- Pictures shall not infer that low forms of sex relationship are the accepted or common thing.
- Obscenity in word, gesture, reference, song, joke, or by suggestion (even when likely to be understood only by part of the audience) is forbidden.
- Undressing scenes should be avoided and never used except when they're essential to the plot.
- Indecent or undue exposure is forbidden. Dancing or costumes intended to permit undue exposure or indecent movement in a dance are forbidden, as well as dances suggesting or representing sexual actions or indecent passions.
- Homosexuality and bestiality are banned.
- Drug use (including alcohol consumption) is banned unless the plot calls for it. Drug use is only allowed if the story is a cautionary tale against drug abuse or if the druggie gets what he or she deserved for taking drugs in the first place.

Portions of the code seemed almost tailor-made to tamp down many of Betty's most popular cartoons. "The institution of marriage and the home shall be upheld," the code decreed. "Scenes of passion should not be introduced when not essential to the plot. Excessive and lustful kissing, lustful embracing, suggestive postures and gestures, are not to be shown. Indecent or undue exposure is forbidden," and so on.

A Betty Boop fan reading these portions of the code for the first time might well have been forgiven for dropping dead in his or her theater seat. To make things worse, Hays, Breen, and the other administrators appointed to enforce these new regulations were definitely not fans of Betty's minimalist outfits and her overwhelmingly flirtatious behavior.

After enforcement of the code began in 1934, no film or cartoon could be released without the Production Code Seal of Approval. This had a major effect on Betty's personality and appearance. The Fleischers were forced to animate her with longer skirts, abandon her hoop earrings and her garter, and no longer show her winking suggestively and wiggling her hips. Pre-code, she had done exactly this in the opening credits of almost every cartoon she made. After the code was in force, her cleavage was always covered, with her outfit always buttoned up to the collar, and other characters could no longer fondle any part of her anatomy. Betty often wore a lace apron as well, and animators began drawing her as older and somewhat heavier. Most of the curls on top of her head were also eliminated, though this was allegedly done to save animation time.

Soon afterward, Betty began costarring in cartoons with Grampy, a bald, white-bearded crackpot inventor who ingeniously solved Betty's domestic problems by inventing and building amazing mechanical devices that he created from existing objects. He was seen as too old to be sexually involved with her and, as his nickname implied, might even have been a relative of hers. (Betty and Grampy are shown kissing each other, but non-romantically, in the cartoon "Be Human," released on November 20, 1936.) It's also possible he was supposed to be related to Koko the Clown, judging from the shape of his head and his black Koko-like nose. Unfortunately for Betty, the Fleischers decided to make Grampy the hero of most of the cartoons in which he and Betty starred while reducing Betty to a weak and helpless woman. That was certainly not how she'd originally been conceived.

The cartoon "Betty and Grampy," released on August 16, 1935, offers a good demonstration of how Grampy functioned in these cartoons. While Betty is home alone one day, she receives a letter from Grampy inviting her to "come right over" to a party at his house and

Betty and Grampy in "Zula Hula" (1937).

asking her to "bring the gang." The decision to have Grampy invite Betty to bring friends is odd, since at this stage in her life, she didn't seem to have any. But in this cartoon, she proves hardly the type to let that stop her from attending. It is still broad daylight when she leaves her house to go over to Grampy's, and numerous men who are working outdoors notice the young, attractive woman strutting along the street. They undoubtedly also hear the song she is singing about how great the party at Grampy's is going to be. Two piano movers, a firefighter, and a traffic cop abandon their assigned tasks and are soon marching and singing behind Betty.

Although Grampy is napping in the chaise lounge in his living room when they arrive, he immediately admits his five guests and shows them the huge cake and large bowl of punch he's prepared. The guests immediately sample both and find them delightful. When they ask him for music, he hooks various household implements together to play the song "Tiger Rag," also known as "Hold That Tiger." The Fleischers obviously loved this song: they'd also featured it in Betty's 1932 "Minnie the Moocher" cartoon. Despite his age, Grampy dances a very vigorous solo in his spats while the song plays. Betty, still wearing her high heels, also bounces around very energetically as the cartoon unreels. Soon, Grampy and Betty are dancing as a couple, while the other guests also pair off. Even after everyone else is too tired to continue, Grampy keeps dancing on his own until he, too, collapses into a chair. Apart from having been inspired to follow Betty to the party in the first place, no romance between her and the men is suggested.

In other cartoons, Betty does have love interests, but they too have shifted. The Fleischers grew increasingly nervous about Betty's long on-screen love affair with dog-man Bimbo, given that bestiality was specifically forbidden by the Production Code. This led to Bimbo's replacement in 1934 by a fully human character, Freddie (also known as "Fearless Fred") in "She Wronged Him Right," released on January 5 of that year. The cartoon in part lampoons the roles of silent movie star Pearl White. White had started her career as a stage actress and later starred in so many film serials that she had become known as "Queen of the Serials." She often did her own stunts on-screen, especially in the popular movie series "The Perils of Pauline." White raced cars, flew airplanes, and swam across rivers, making her unlike most female stars of the day, but somewhat like Betty.

"She Wronged Him Right" finds Betty starring in a local stage production of a Victorian-style melodrama with the same title. Betty plays a woman who can't pay the mortgage on her single-family farm. While the production's plotline is inescapably melodramatic, this was a very realistic situation in America during the Great Depression. Between 1929 and 1933, the four years preceding the release of this cartoon, one-third of all American farmers lost their farms because the plummeting prices for crops and livestock left them unable to make their mortgage payments. Less realistically, but certainly in formulaic congruence with theatrical dramas over the previous hundred years or so, Betty's mortgage is about to be collected not by a stolid or perhaps embarrassed representative of the bank to which she owes the money, but by a Snidely Whiplash–type villain appropriately named "Heeza Rat."

Betty's reputation as a flirt had made her the perfect actress for such a part. When Heeza demands her mortgage payment, Betty's character makes a show of putting her hand down one of her stockings to search for the money, although even one bill, much less the pile of greenbacks needed to make her mortgage payment, would have been hard to conceal. In deference to the alleged sensitivities of legitimate theater patrons, however, when she takes the obligatory next step of searching for the booty in her bodice, she modestly turns her back on the audience before doing so. Heeza watches Betty search for the money with rapturous interest, and when, to no one's surprise, she's unable to find any, Heeza moves right on to the next step, which is to suggestively propose that she pay in another way.

Unlike her previous admirers, however, Heeza refrains from stroking Betty's legs or groping her. In fact, he takes the high road, such as it is, professing his love for her and telling her how much younger she looks every day. Perhaps impressed by Heeza's politesse, Betty's character's immediate response is to indicate her openness to the idea. Instead of looking shocked or insulted, Betty sings about how she needs jewelry and hair ribbons. As we all know, these cost money. Heeza then makes his big mistake, however, and tells her he wants her to be his wife. Betty's character immediately breaks into tears. She'd been running the farm on her own before. Why split the profits now? Losing patience, Heeza picks her up while she pounds him with her little fists. "If Fearless Fred were only here," she cries as the curtain descends.

This was the Fleischers' way of introducing Freddy, Betty's new and fully human boyfriend, and a replacement for Bimbo in her affections. In the play's next scene, it is made clear to the audience that the character Freddy is playing on stage is not only a strong handsome lumberjack, but also the owner of the Fearless Fred Lumber Company. When he hears Betty's cry for help, he naturally sets out to rescue her. He arrives on the scene to find that Heeza has tied her to a stake in a tank that is filling with water. He beats up Heeza and rescues Betty, who embraces him and calls him "My hero."

Freddy, shown here in the 1934 cartoon "She Wronged Him Right" as the owner of the Fearless Fred Lumber Company.

Meanwhile, Betty's animal companions, like her cute new moon-faced dog Pudgy, were almost entirely mute and acted like pets rather than men. And while Betty clearly has enormous affection for Pudgy, it is obviously the love of a pet owner, without romantic overtones. Keeping in mind that Betty had once sported canine features herself, she went, in the words of one wag, from being part dog to being upstaged by her own pooch. The doglike Bimbo had been taller than Betty and spent much of his time walking on two legs, talking, singing, playing games, and generally acting like a human being. Pudgy, by contrast, was 100 percent dog and about the size of a small baby, which also made a certain sense; had Betty been open to marriage, perhaps by this time she would have had a child of her own.

In "Betty Boop's Little Pal" cartoon, released September 21, 1934, she takes Pudgy on a picnic to a nearby park. "I don't need the sunshine when I'm blue, all I need is just a smile from you," she sings to him as they set out to spend the day in the park together. Betty emphasizes her love for Pudgy by bringing a huge basket of food with them to the park, which she begins unpacking as soon as they arrive. It includes a full-sized cake and several other dishes—much too much food for the two of them, which recalls Betty's own parents trying to overfeed her in 1932's "Minnie the Moocher."

As Pudgy is a pup at this point rather than a mature dog, however, he begins to misbehave right after gobbling down the Jell-O. First, he fights with Betty over a string of sausages, causing her to fall flat on her face into her carefully prepared cake. Next, he activates a seltzer bottle with his paws and sprays Betty in the face with it. An infuriated Betty spanks him and tells him to go home. Pudgy begins padding sadly homeward but has walked only a few feet before being

Pudgy made his first appearance in "Betty Boop's Little Pal" (1934).

nabbed by the local dogcatcher. Extremely alarmed and overcome with guilt, Betty races after the dogcatcher's van. When she catches up with it, she tearfully sings "What will I do now we're apart?" to Pudgy through the van's wire mesh cage, and he sobs piteously in response. Shortly thereafter, Pudgy and some other dogs manage to escape from the van, and Pudgy returns to Betty's arms. Subdued, he swiftly regains his good cheer as Betty sings lovingly to him about how he'll always be hers.

In general, Betty acts much more like a well-mannered housewife than an aggressive flirt in the cartoons of this period. As another critic put it, Betty had become a homebody, in the sense of caring more about her home than her body. Betty's ambitions also seemed to have changed. During the first part of her cartoon life, it looks as though she might become a great actress, or even president of the United States. Post–Hays Code, however, she's depicted in more stereotypical jobs like nurse, teacher, and babysitter.

Neither the Fleischers nor Betty's animators were happy about this. On several occasions, they rebelled. In one of Betty's later cartoons, "A Language All My Own," which was released on July 19, 1935, she sings the title song in both English and Japanese to a Japanese audience. While the English version would have put a choir boy to sleep, the Japanese version included the phrase, "Come to bed with me and we'll boop-oop-a-doop," probably waking up a few tired-out Tokyo moviegoers.

The Fleischers occasionally allowed themselves to violate the Hays Code more pointedly when it came to nonsexual content. Many of the code's provisions dealt with on-screen violence, for instance. The code forbade, in part:

- third-degree methods;
- brutality and possible gruesomeness;
- branding of people or animals; and
- apparent cruelty to both children and animals.

Such behavior had been almost totally absent from Betty's cartoons previously. In reaction to the code's restrictions on lasciviousness, however, the Fleischers decided to make a cartoon that would flagrantly violate the code's restrictions on brutality. Amazingly, they got away with it, probably because the cartoon not only showed the brutal conduct in great detail but then showed the same brutality being applied to the original inflictor, thus gratifying the Hays Code's Puritan lust for revenge.

In this cartoon, somewhat mockingly titled "Be Human" and released November 20, 1936, Betty, wearing a respectable dress, is in her living room playing the piano and singing the cartoon's title song. As she sings "Be human, animals can cry . . . / Have a tender place for every animal and bird," she hears and sees her neighbor, a large, muscular farmer, through her open window. He is viciously whipping a small, yelping dog leashed to a stake. Betty pleads with the farmer to stop, but he ignores her. He keeps whipping the pup, and then punches a cow in the face for providing no milk and brutalizes a chicken for providing no eggs.

Knowing that Grampy runs his own local animal aid society, Betty telephones him for help. (Grampy's phone adds to the already brutal atmosphere by waking him from a nap with several punches to the face. The Fleischer animators must have been having a bad week when they created this cartoon.) Grampy motors frantically to the scene in

A more domesticated post–Hays Code Betty appeared in "Be Human" (1936).

his animal aid society van, catching the farmer in the act of whipping a horse. He immediately shoves the farmer into his van, which includes a mobile jail cell, and drives back to the aid society with his prisoner. Once there and joined by Betty, he dumps the farmer into a cellar where a mechanized whip lashes him while he tries to escape via a conveyor belt. The energy that is thus generated powers machines that shake apples from a tree for hogs to gobble, release fodder for a cow to eat, and milk a cow for the benefit of hungry cats. Betty and Grampy keep laughing sadistically while apparently enjoying his suffering.

According to at least one reviewer, it was clear that the cartoon had violated the Hays code. Among the transgressions they noted were "(1) Man brutally whipping a horse and dog; (2) Man punching a cow; (3) Man wringing the neck of a live chicken; (4) Abusive man being horsewhipped as retribution; and (5) Man laughing while animals suffer." There's no record of any Hays official ever complaining, however.

Max Fleischer also found another way to express frustration with the Hays Code. In August 1934, he struck back as best he could via the newspaper comic strip in which Betty was also appearing. In Fleischer's first anti-Hays strip, which appeared in September 1934, he had Betty tell her director that because of this "clean-up-the-movies thing," her lawyers have insisted on passing on all her scripts. Exasperated, the director shows Betty a big pile of scripts the studio has purchased for her, noting that "We paid thousands for these classics." He assembles Betty's attorneys in his office and asks them if "there's any story you mugs will okay for Betty" under the code. Their response is to show him the only script they can approve, which they claim to have written themselves. Its title is "Little Miss Muffet"—obviously based on the innocuous eighteenth-century poem.

Shortly thereafter, in another of Betty's comic strips, the director tells her there are scenes and dialogue in her next movie that her lawyers are examining at that very moment. Two hours later, the attorneys emerge from their conference room to announce that the only portion of the movie they'll allow to be produced is its theme song. And in a subsequent strip, Betty satirizes what her lawyers are doing by using a mop and broom to clean up the set of her next picture. This ruins it, in her director's estimation: the movie had been titled "Sally of the Slums."

A different form of resistance to the newly domesticated Betty did not come from the Fleischers at all. Neither they nor any other reputable creators were about to release truly sexually explicit stories about Betty in either filmed or printed form, but various anonymous others saw opportunity in doing so. Among those fans were the writers, illustrators, and publishers of a series of pornographic publications in the 1930s informally called "Tijuana Bibles." In these comic books, male and female movie, cartoon, comic strip, and comic book stars engaged in detailed sex acts with random partners. All these comic books certainly violated then-current obscenity laws, in addition to infringing their original creators' copyrights. In one such 1935 comic, titled *Betty Steps Out* and written by the pseudonymous "Regina Doosh," Betty takes up prostitution and has explicit sex with such equally well-known male cartoon characters as Barney Google, Jiggs, Moon Mullins, and Joe Palooka, as well as her fellow Fleischer creation, Popeye. In one from 1936 by "Ima Pushover" and titled "Improvising," Betty plays the ukulele while exploring a variety of sexual positions with an attractive male lifeguard.

The Code ruled Hollywood for the next thirty-four years. In the years following World War II, however, imports of European books

Cover of a 1936 "Tijuana Bible" featuring Betty titled "Improvising."

and films and the general liberalization of American society made the code less and less popular, and filmmakers began to rebel. When the film *The Moon Is Blue* was released without a seal of approval in 1953, the code began losing its power. The film portrayed William Holden and David Niven playing rivals for the favors of a young woman played by Maggie McNamara. During the movie, Ms. McNamara accepts a $600 gift from Niven, and kisses him while wearing Holden's bathrobe in Holden's apartment.

By 1959, the power of the code was largely broken, and Betty symbolically pardoned for her past behavior, when Marilyn Monroe's performance of Helen Kane's song and Betty's inspiration, "I Wanna Be Loved by You" in the movie *Some Like It Hot* was greeted with more praise than damnation. Monroe even inserted Betty's catchphrase, "Boop-oop-a-doop" into the song in an apparent tribute to Betty.

That scene features, among other things, Monroe in a revealing outfit and actors Jack Lemmon and Tony Curtis wearing wigs and women's clothing while playing instruments in the orchestra. If the Hays Code couldn't stop a movie like that, it couldn't stop anything. In fact, the film received six Academy Award nominations, including Best Actor, Best Director, and Best Adapted Screenplay.

Seven years later, in 1968, the code aimed at censoring movies such as *Some Like It Hot* would be replaced by a film rating system that assigned labels such as "G," "PG," and "R" to films to define their intended audience. Still, the code had damaged Betty's cartoon and comic strip career by vastly reducing her sex appeal. It also had seriously damaged the Fleischers' business model: during the years prior to the consistent enforcement of the Hays Code, Betty had been more popular than Pudgy, Grampy, and all their other new characters combined.

7

WHO BOOPED FIRST?

The Hays Code was not the only obstacle the Fleischers were facing. Aside from Betty's open expressions of sexuality, which got her into trouble with the censors, another major kink in her career was that the Fleischers had modeled parts of her personality on real-life actress Helen Kane, who in turn had drawn on the performances of Esther Lee Jones, Florence Mills, and other African American entertainers.

Jones, also known as "Little Esther" or "Baby Esther," was born in 1918. By the late 1920s, even as a child star, Jones had become well-known in Harlem and throughout the world for using scat phrases such as "Boo-Boo-Boo," "Wha-Da-Da," and "Doo-Doo-Doo" in her performances. Certainly, she didn't invent scat: Louis Armstrong had recorded one of the first scat songs, "Heebie Jeebies," in 1926. Cab Calloway, who appeared in three Betty Boop cartoons during the early 1930s, used scat so often he came to be known as "The Hi De Ho Man" after one of his own variations. Later performers would do the same: vocalist Sara Vaughn, for instance, would sing "shoo-doo-shoo-bee-ooo-bee-doo" in the 1940s, and, twenty-five years after Betty's

Esther Lee Jones began her performing career while still a child. Here she appears on the front cover of a 1929 issue of *Vu*, a French weekly.

birth, Little Richard began his 1955 hit song "Tutti Frutti" with the scat phrase "A wop-bop-a-lu-bop-a-lop-bam-boom!"

Jones herself had started her career impersonating Florence Mills, a 1920s African American stage and singing star who was noted for her use of phrases such as "too-ty-tooty-to." Using her imitations of Mills as a launching pad, Jones's career prospered to such an extent that she toured Europe in 1929, performing for King Alphonso and Queen Victoria Eugenie of Spain and King Gustave of Sweden. Later, she also sang in several countries in South America.

This became a matter of interest to Betty Boop's creators, competitors, and fans because Kane, who was white, had visited the Everglades Club in New

Little Esther started her career impersonating Florence Mills, shown here in a 1923 photograph. AGENCE ROL PHOTO COURTESY BIBLIOTHÈQUE NATIONALE DE FRANCE / WIKIMEDIA COMMONS USER L'ANGE AU SOURIRE.

York and saw Jones's act in 1928. Kane's career had taken off the year before. At that time, she was appearing in a successful Broadway musical called *A Night in Spain*. It ran for a total of 174 performances at Manhattan's 44th Street Theatre and earned rave reviews that landed Kane a gig at the Paramount Theater, a definite move up in theater world.

Determined to keep rising, Kane inserted the scat lyric "boop-boop-a-doop" into the song "That's My Weakness Now," and sang it on stage. The change worked its magic, and Kane was soon on her way to the top. A short while later she was earning $5,000 a week, a large sum now and a mind-boggling weekly wage in 1928. Realizing how powerful the magical phrase "boop-boop-a-doop" had become, Kane also inserted it into the recorded version of "I Wanna Be Loved By You" released by Victor Records that same year. As Kane's stage and recording career continued and her popularity skyrocketed, she used the same phrase so often that she became known as the "Boop-Oop-a-Doop Girl."

Kane had long resented what she considered to be Betty's theft of her catchphrase. But she was thrown for a loop in April 1932 when she saw Betty playing a fur-crazed sexpot in the cartoon "A-Hunting We Will Go." This wasn't the sort of behavior Kane wished to be associated with. She also couldn't help noticing how popular Betty was becoming as Helen's own career was starting to level off. Something had to be done.

One month after "A-Hunting" was released, Kane filed a $250,000 suit (the equivalent of a $5 million suit in 2023) against Max Fleischer, Fleischer Studios, and Paramount, the Fleischer Studios' distributor. Kane claimed that Betty had substantially reduced her popularity by stealing her personality and exhibiting it as her own on-screen. Kane had no idea what a major event her suit would become when it actually came to trial two years later in April 1934.

For the press at this point, during the fourth month of the sixth year of the Great Depression, a public fight between two famous and attractive women—one real, one animated—was the perfect respite from stories about layoffs, breadlines, and budget cuts. Snapping to attention, numerous jaded New York journalists flocked to cover the case. Even before the trial began, one writer anticipated it with a fictional imagining of how Kane would testify that appeared in several newspapers:

Attorney: Now then, on what occasion did you first sing this song?

Kane: I sang it on any and all occasions.

Attorney: Would you mind singing it so the judge can hear it?

Kane: Not at all. It goes like this . . . Boop-oop-a-doop! Boop-oop-a-doop! Boop-oop-a- doop!

Judge: Let me see if I understand you clearly. You say it goes like this . . . Boop-oop-a- doop! Boop-oop-a-doop! Boop-oop-a-doop!

Kane: That's it, your honor.

Judge: I just want to be certain of the facts. I'd hate to be over-ruled by the Supreme Court through an error in the exact number of "boop-oop-a-doops" or their proper sequence. Only last month one of our leading jurists was overruled in a song suit involving the number of "hey-nonnie-nonnies" in a song called 'Hot Cha-Cha.' Glotz versus Bernstein, I think it was.

For the buttoned-up citizenry of the 1930s, the real beginning of the trial was nearly as entertaining. When Kane took the stand to testify, her attorney, Samuel Robert Weltz, asked her to remove her coat and hat. This was quite an unusual request in an era when ladies kept all their clothes on at formal occasions, and a public trial in New York County Supreme Court was definitely formal.

The reporters covering the trial assumed, correctly, that Weltz wished to demonstrate how much Kane's fully revealed face and lightly clothed figure resembled Betty's. After partly disrobing his client, he then expanded verbally on a brief he'd filed earlier with the court. That document quoted from a long list of advertisements, newspaper stories, and proclamations that Weltz contended proved that Betty was stealing many of her mannerisms from Kane, including the much talked-about "boop-oop-a-doop" phrase. According to him, those stolen mannerisms included "coyness," "pouting of the lips," "rolling of the eyes," and other gestures. He showed the court numerous photos backing up his claims.

Folks, meet Betty Boop (right). You'll be seeing a lot of her because she is the new animated cartoon character who is trying to cut in on Mickey Mouse's popularity. Does she look familiar to you? Now look at little boop-a-dooper Helen Kane. Helen was the cartoonist's inspiration for Betty, the first time a real life character has been used for the popular jumping comics

The Kane trial attracted considerable media attention. This comparison of Kane and Betty appeared in the April 1, 1932, issue of the magazine *Photoplay*.
COURTESY INTERNET ARCHIVE / WIKIMEDIA COMMONS USER BATFAN 1966.

Members of the courtroom audience, already amused by the general subject of the trial, were even more entertained by the fact that Kane was wearing a flaming red hat decorated with a long brown feather that tickled her attorney's ear each time he bent over to confer with her.

Weltz continued to make headway, however, by pointing out that the Fleischers had explicitly used Kane's name and picture for commercial purposes in Betty's "Stopping the Show" cartoon. Released on August 12, 1932, that cartoon had shown Betty on stage imitating other performers, including Fanny Brice and Maurice Chevalier, and drawings of their faces had appeared on an easel Betty was sharing the stage with. Weltz noted that in Betty's first scene in the cartoon, Betty was originally shown copying Kane's actual vaudeville act. That scene had been cut from the cartoon after Kane filed her suit against the Fleischers. Weltz noted, however, that despite that cut, Kane's likeness appeared twice in the cartoon on the easel.

Kane testified about her own Betty-like appearance and use of the phrase "boop-oop-a-doop" in several films, including *Sweetie*, *Good Boy*, *Pointed Heels*, and *Dangerous Nan McGrew*. She went on to emphasize Betty's use of the phrase "boop-oop-a-doop" in many cartoons and then denounced Betty for singing a song called "Dangerous Nan McGrew" in the "Bum Bandit" cartoon. Weltz then convinced the judge, Edward J. McGoldrick, to watch the cartoon in question. Courtroom spectators, news reporters, and court officers joined McGoldrick in watching the screening with great interest.

Things sure looked bad for Betty. Many courtroom observers were certain that the Fleischers were on the verge of losing the suit. Then the defense began.

Fleischer attorney N. William Welling's first step was to call for the testimony of five women who'd provided Betty with their voices to use on screen. Each one of them—Little Ann Little, Margie Hines, Kate Wright, Bonnie Poe, and Mae Questel—took the stand in turn to deny

In Kane's suit against the Fleischers, her lawyers pointed out that the cartoon "Bum Bandit" co-opted the character name "Dangerous Nan McGrew" from Kane's 1930 movie. In this lobby poster, Kane is notably identified as "The Boop-Boopa-Doop Girl."

ever having tried to imitate Kane as well as to demonstrate their own individual singing styles.

Little Ann Little testified that early in the 1920s, she'd been singing in a similar style in Greenwich Village nightclubs. She went on to tell the court how "boop-oop-a-doop" allegedly had started out as "ba-da-in-de-do," developed into "bo-do-de-o-do," and finally became "boop-oop-a-doop."

According to the *New York Times*, Little spoke continuously in a high-pitched voice that closely resembled Betty's. Weltz, Kane's attorney, annoyed by what he considered fakery, sarcastically asked Little "Do you talk that way at home?" causing the crowd to burst into guffaws. Far from intimidated, Little replied in a high-pitched voice, "Yes indeedy!"

While arguing over whether these women had Betty singing in their own original styles or merely imitating Kane, the attorneys spent the next several days dissecting and comparing each woman's use of the syllables involved. On several occasions, the attorneys and witnesses tried to analyze the differences between "boop-oop-a-doop," "boop-boop-a-doop," "boop-oopy-doop," "boo-boo-be-do, "poo-poopy-do," and "poop-poopy-do-do." After one long session devoted to these phrases, the uptight court stenographer announced that he couldn't handle any more such testimony. He threw his hands in the air and said he'd need help spelling these "meaningless sounds," after which someone went to assist him. The high level of interest in this trial can be gauged by the fact that the stenographer's fit was actually covered in a separate story in the *Times,* under the screaming headline: "Help! Stenographer Can't Take 'Wha-da-da's' and 'Boops.'"

(In obedience to Sigmund Freud's dictate that there are no coincidences, this scene had been partially foreshadowed in the cartoon "Hot Dog" that the Fleischers had released in 1930, four years previously. In that cartoon Bimbo had been arrested on a traffic charge and was testifying in his own defense in court. He testified partly by singing a song and as he sang the words "doo-ey-a-doo-doo, e ya doodle e-doo," a court stenographer typed those words on a sheet of paper headed "TESTIMONY.")

Welling, the Fleischers' attorney, then called Max Fleischer to the stand. Fleischer insisted that Betty was not based on Helen Kane or any other star or character and that she was, in fact, a product of his own imagination. Some giggling was heard in the courtroom when Fleischer said this. Everyone with even a minor interest in the subject was aware that Kane had become a big star in 1927 when she added the scat phrase to "That's My Weakness Now."

Also, Betty obviously looked and acted like Kane. Of course, Kane also resembled Clara Bow and several other pouting female stars of the day. In fact, Kane and Bow had set the standard for the era's coveted female look. Millions of young women in the 1930s wanted to be just like them. Hundreds of Helen Kane Impersonation Competitions (also known as "Boop-Boop-A-Doop" contests) were held throughout the country. Underlying the desire to look like Kane was a widespread wish in the depressed 1930s to return to the 1920s, the decade of the flappers, when girls sported "boyish" bobs and spit curls, and men seemed to be attracted to round female faces, wide, mascaraed eyes, and squeaky voices.

The young women of the 1930s, however, were very serious, and not at all carefree about conforming to this image. When Kane's lawyer had called her to the stand at the beginning of the trial and directed her to take off her hat and coat so the court might see that her face and figure resembled Betty's, Kane, trying to make her resemblance to Betty more striking, rearranged her hair across her temples and cheeks. A male *New York Times* reporter covering the trial was amused to see several young women in the audience immediately do the same.

After the testimony by Betty's voicers, Welling argued that the real question was, who booped first? Kane, Betty, or someone else? His argument was that if Betty was imitating someone other than Kane, Kane didn't deserve to win her suit, because she was the only plaintiff. It was at this point that Lou Bolton, Baby Esther's manager, testified that in 1928, Kane had seen Baby Esther perform at the Everglades Club. He'd not only seen his client, Jones, do her "boop" thing, but had watched Kane watch Jones from the audience. He said he'd even gone over to Kane's table to say hello. (Jones, who was performing in Louisville, Kentucky, at the time of the trial, was not summoned to testify.)

Attorney Welling then asked Bolton what sounds Jones made on stage. Bolton answered: "Boo-Boo-Boo!" Welling then asked him what other sounds Jones made. Bolton answered: "Doo-Doo-Doo." When Walton repeated his question, Bolton said, "Wha-Da-Da-Da." In a case like this, such testimony was key.

Called back to the stand, Kane naturally denied ever seeing Jones do her boop thing. Unfortunately for her, however, Welling then brought a sound film into court and showed it to the judge and everyone else in the courtroom. It was an early talkie that actually showed Jones performing her act on stage in 1928. Many of the courtroom spectators, who'd been brought up on silent films, were amazed that they could actually hear Jones's voice when she sang "boop-boop-a-doop."

The combination of Bolton's testimony and the courtroom's general amazement at the Jones sound film won the day for Betty and the Fleischers. On May 5, 1934, Judge McGoldrick ruled for the defendants, saying that the "baby" technique of singing "did not originate with Miss Kane." The Fleischers had won the battle for ownership of Betty's character and would not have to pay Kane the $250,000 she had demanded.

Having triumphed in their real-life struggle with Helen Kane, the Fleischers couldn't resist rubbing it in, running a victory lap, and taking advantage of the massive publicity the trial had received by titling Betty's next cartoon "Betty Boop's Trial," although the cartoon had no connection to the Kane trial other than its title and outcome. The Fleischers released it on June 15, 1934, six weeks after they'd won their real-life courtroom struggle against Kane. At the beginning of the cartoon, Betty is driving along happily in her new sports car, unaware that a policeman named Freddy is monitoring the road. She then inadvertently drives so close to him, going so fast, that he begins chasing her. Roaring after Betty on his motorcycle, Officer Freddy calls out to her that she is a "beauty" and tells her, "I'd like to know ya." Betty accuses him of being "fresh," and drives away even faster.

When Freddy finally pulls her over, he asks to see her license. Betty responds by standing up on the driver's seat and extending one of her legs over the windshield and onto the hood to show a license plate hanging from her garter. She has no driver's license, however, so Freddy lifts her onto the handlebars of his motorcycle and drives her right into the courtroom where her trial is to take place. (Miraculously, no one there seems concerned that Freddy's motorcycle is belching exhaust into the court.) Betty, after complaining that she is a working girl and the court is wasting her time, immediately pleads guilty. She and Freddy then sing a scat duet in front of the judge and jury about how attracted they are to each other. Rather than citing both Betty and Freddy for contempt, the cartoon judge merely notes Betty's physical assets in the court record: "Blue eyes, nice form, cute legs, and miscellaneous." After Betty winks and blushes at the all-male jury, they vote her not guilty 12–0. In response, she performs another impromptu dance, and everyone else in the courtroom joins in. Freddy then lifts her onto the back of his motorbike and drives her away. The two of them appear to be enjoying themselves immensely. Case closed. Once again, Betty had prevailed in court. Freddy would make a number of appearances in subsequent cartoons as a love interest.

Meanwhile, Helen Kane had been preparing her own media version of the Betty Boop trial. For obvious reasons, Kane's take on the trial was much nastier than the Fleischers' had been. Kane's version was released on June 21, 1934, six days after the release of the "Betty Boop's Trial" cartoon, as part of the weekly radio program "The Fleischmann's Yeast Hour," hosted by popular singer Rudy Vallee. After Vallee and Kane had each sung several songs to open the episode, the entire cast took part in a musical comedy about the suit. At one point, Kane says, "I want a pound of Fleischer!" an obvious reference to the Jewish moneylender Shylock's demand for a pound of flesh from Antonio the debtor in Shakespeare's *The Merchant of Venice*. (If Kane had spouted this line in this context more recently, she might have been accused of gross anti-Semitism.) Kane's statement also arguably worked as a more subtle pun: *Fleischer* and *Fleischmann* both mean "butcher" in German.

Helen Kane and Betty Boop would face off one more time in a completely different venue: comic strips. In July 1934, Betty had begun appearing in numerous newspapers in a daily King Features strip. Kane, after losing her suit, decided to strike back by suggesting that King Features do a comic strip based on *her* rather than Betty. King ultimately signed a short-term contract with Kane and artist Ving Fuller to begin drawing a Sunday full-color, full-page Helen Kane comic strip titled "The Original Boop-Boop-A-Doop Girl by Helen Kane." This strip appeared in the *New York Mirror* newspaper every Sunday beginning in August of 1934, less than a month after Betty's daily strip had premiered.

The first strip concerns a theft from Kane of $560, a very large amount of money at the time. The theft has been committed by a large bald man wearing a red and yellow horizontally striped shirt who'd stolen the money by managing to fool Kane into signing a check that she'd thought was a page in an autograph book. After the culprit is arrested and jailed, Kane goes to visit him, and when the man claims to still "worship" her autograph, she gives him another one, signed "Boop-Boop-a-Doop" rather than "Helen Kane." It seemed an obvious attempt by Kane to reassert her claim to being the original "Boop-Boop-a-Doop" girl.

Kane returned to this theme in her fourth strip when, once again, a thief attempts to steal a large amount of money from her. He breaks into her apartment while she is counting her cash and takes it from her. Kane, however, tries to convince him that she's been counting stage money, not the real thing. The thief is so impressed by her intelligence and looks that he offers her a job in his gang of criminals and the opportunity to be his girlfriend. After Kane pretends to accept, she goes into her bedroom supposedly to change clothes, and calls the police on her bedroom phone to have him arrested.

The first strip of Helen Kane's short-lived comic appeared on August 26, 1934.

So, for the second time in one month, in her comic strip at least, Kane had fought back against two different thieves, both of them apparent stand-ins for the Fleischers, after they'd attempted to steal a large amount of money from her. Nonetheless, in real life, Kane's strip expired in the fall and was not renewed, while Betty would soon have her own full-color, full-page Sunday strip, which would run for three years. The Fleischers had won again.

8

BETTY OFF-SCREEN

Betty's comic strip was not the Fleischers' only attempt to make their most successful creation into a true multimedia personality. In 1932, they tried their hand at making her a radio star as well as a comic strip and animated cartoon character. That was the year the radio show "The Betty Boop Fables" premiered. Also known as "The Betty Boop Film Fables," "The Betty Boop Frolics," "Betty Boop's Gang," "Betty Boop and Her Pals," and "Betty Boop on the Air," depending on which local station carried the program, it was broadcast on the NBC Radio Network for fifteen minutes every Tuesday evening starting November 15, 1932. Max Fleischer directed the show and sometimes appeared on it as "the Director," which was somewhat odd because Dave Fleischer was always credited as the director of Betty's cartoons.

William "Billy" Costello, also known as "Red Pepper Sam," also was heard on the show using the raspy voice he'd provided Ferdinand "Freddie" Frog, a character in several of Betty's cartoons. Costello's excellent performance eventually earned him the job of voicer for

Popeye. Bonnie Poe, Mae Questel, Little Ann Little, and Margie Hines also performed on the show, voicing Betty.

The appropriately named Bradley Barker voiced Bimbo. Earlier, he'd also voiced such other minor Betty Boop cartoon characters as Kasper Kangaroo, Molly Mule, Gus Gorilla, and Samson Mouse, the latter being an early attempt by the Fleischers to compete with Disney's Mickey Mouse. Barker had been a movie actor and director during the 1920s and also had provided the sound of the MGM Lion on-screen before that studio substituted a real lion's roar for Barker's.

One reviewer called the "Betty Boop Fables Show" a "mad skit" and noted that during the broadcast, Betty's voicers sometimes imitated Jeanie Lang, an actress and singer who'd starred in the 1932 movie *King of Jazz*. Meanwhile, that same reviewer also opined that Costello, the voicer for Ferdinand Frog, did double duty by imitating popular entertainer Poley McClintock, who sang in a low, frog-like croak while he was a drummer in Fred Waring's Pennsylvanians jazz band.

Another reviewer called the show's quarter-hour "entirely devoted to music and nonsense," and added that "what little dialogue finds its way in between vocal and orchestral numbers is entirely in rhyme." Vic Irwin's Band, which provided the music for many of Betty's cartoons, provided the music for her radio show as well.

On one representative episode, sworn enemies Gus Gorilla and Kasper Kangaroo battle it out while Freddie Frog referees their fight and Betty sings in the background. One reviewer noted that Gus Gorilla had the advantage of a long reach while Kasper's tail had a mean swing, and another said that "when Gus Gorilla gives a grunt it's enough to make shivers run up and down your spine." Despite such praise, the show never achieved the heights of popularity that Betty had reached in her cartoons. It was broadcast for only nine weeks before being canceled in January 1933.

Betty's comic strips would prove more successful. In 1933, Fleischer Studios had initiated negotiations with the King Features syndicate to produce and release a daily black-and-white comic strip as well as a weekly full-page color comic strip, appearing on Sundays, about Betty's adventures in Hollywood, both to be drawn by artist Bud Counihan. The negotiations for the Sunday strip dragged on and on, while her daily strip began appearing in numerous newspapers on July 23, 1934, and ran for eight months, until March 30, 1935. Once the Sunday version began, however, it ran much longer than Betty's daily strip, appearing from November 25, 1934, through November 28, 1937.

At the same time that Betty's manner and job choices were becoming more conservative in her cartoons, due to the strictures of the Production Code, the comic strips showed her living the life of a flamboyant Hollywood star. And, while her behavior was not as dramatic as that of some modern-day stars, she very quickly began acting like a diva, although a relatively subtle one. She attempted to get her way mostly through inaction, strategically arranged accidents, and humor.

In one of Betty's early strips, cameramen are gathered to film her for a scene in which she is supposed to be sleeping. However, because she actually falls asleep during filming and her contract forbids anyone from disturbing her until she is awake, everyone is forced to wait by her bedside until the next day to begin shooting again. In another strip, her throat is sprayed and resprayed, instruments are tested and retested, and other extensive preparations are made over a period of hours so she can speak one word—"Boop!"—into a microphone for a movie soundtrack. Other strips depict film crews having to wear blindfolds while shooting her in a skimpy swimsuit, and waiting for hours while she looks for a garter she has misplaced.

The strips also marked the last appearance, at least for several decades, of Freddy, who had been introduced in "Betty Boop's Trial" and appeared as a romantic admirer in a number of her other animated films. In the strip, Freddy makes one more gallant effort to capture her heart, so determined to marry her that he follows her to Hollywood, dyes his hair blond, and buys a nice suit so he can take her to dinner at a fancy Los Angeles restaurant. Shortly after they sit down at the table, however, a huge crowd invades the place, screaming for Betty's autograph. Obviously more interested in pleasing the crowd than in pleasing Freddy, Betty rejects his suggestion that she disguise herself for their next meeting. Disgusted with her behavior, Freddy finally gives up for good, and Betty seems to have jet-propelled herself into life-long single status.

Indeed, Betty's behavior in the comics is not simply that of a spoiled diva. She is also shown to be a canny and career-focused business-woman. In another strip, studio executives have spent months trying to write a movie contract that she'll actually sign. Willing to sacri-fice her feminism in order to maintain control over the process, Betty stalls the negotiations by pretending she thinks they concern contract bridge rather than legal agreements, and telling both sides that she thinks "the party of the first part" is an actual social occasion. When her attorneys tell her that her contract would forbid her from appearing in shorts—meaning short films—she objects by saying "I look cute in shorts." She continues to prolong the negotiations by demanding two six-month vacations every year, claiming she can't sign because she has writer's block, spilling ink all over the contract, and commissioning the construction of a full-size dummy of herself and secretly leaving the room.

Betty is also shown having to deal with Hollywood's beauty standards. In the 1930s those standards had moved on from the archetype of a flat-chested flapper, but, while prominent breasts and hips were acceptable, putting on any weight past that point was verboten. At a time when her industry contemporaries were forced to swallow endless diet pills and amphetamines to keep their weight down, Betty's comic strip movie directors tried other methods to keep her thin. In a comic strip dated September 15, 1934, Betty's director notices that she is gaining weight and begins harassing her about it. "You're overweight, and your contract says you can't go over 100 pounds. You must get some of that avoirdupois off!" he tells her. At first, Betty responds dutifully. The very next day she plays tennis, rides horseback, and swims vigorously, all during one eight-hour shift. Unfortunately, all that exercise makes her hungry, and she ends her workout with a hearty steak dinner at a nearby restaurant. The next day, both Betty and her director are amazed that rather than losing weight, she's gained five pounds.

Within a few days, Betty begins to feel persecuted by her all-male supervisory team and starts fighting back feminist style avant la lettre. When her director asks her if she'd followed the diet he created for her, she says she had, but at her required weigh-in, the scale shows she has again gained weight. When the director asks if she's sure she hasn't eaten anything but the food prescribed in her diet, her response is, "Nothing, er, that is, excepting my ordinary meals!" Betty isn't that stupid, however. Her alleged confusion is her first step in fighting back. A couple of days later, still smarting at the weight-loss regimen being imposed on her, Betty is flabbergasted when her director hands her the script for her next picture, "Dinner for Two." Rather than respond gratefully to the studio's continued interest in keeping her a star, Betty studies the script and tells the director that the restaurant scene will have to be cut from the film. When he protests that that particular scene was the most important part of the picture, Betty says she won't be able to film it because she is on such a strict diet. After several convoluted ploys finally bring Betty's weight down, they film the picture. Shortly afterward she adjourns to the studio cafeteria and orders a banana split smothered with a double portion of whipped cream. When the studio private eye who is following her reports her conduct to her director, her four fat and balding lawyers harrumph over to the cafeteria and tell her that eating fattening foods or drinks is a violation of her contract. Betty's response, as she watches them lumber away, is that they could lose some weight themselves.

Although the strips had dispensed with Freddy, they did introduce several new characters. One was Van Twinkle, a fellow movie star at a neighboring studio who was very clearly intended to be gay. Homosexuality, of course, was a hush-hush subject in the early twentieth century, though its depiction was not entirely unprecedented in the movies. The first erotic kiss between two members of the same sex in a film occurred as early as 1922. But once the Hays Code was in place, the topic was completely off-limits.

Even before Betty has met Van Twinkle in person, she calls him "colossal" and remarks "what a man!" She even considers changing her hair color from brunette to blonde, platinum, or even red, white, and blue to attract him. Meanwhile, she ignores the clear signals Van Twinkle is sending her. When Betty sees him walking down the street in one strip, she pulls the old "drop the handkerchief" trick to attract

Panels from Betty's daily strip of March 18, 1935, featuring the new characters Van Twinkle and Billy.

his attention. His response is to simply pick up the hanky and blow his own nose into it. Betty nevertheless continues to pursue Twinkle relentlessly, even making the mistake at one point of accosting his studio double. When she does meet him again in person, it starts raining and she immediately sees the situation as an opportunity for them to call a taxi and snuggle together in its backseat. Not being a cad, Twinkle flags down a cab, puts her in it, and remains by himself on the sidewalk while it drives away.

After repeated similar incidents, Twinkle gives in and finally takes her out to lunch. While she wants to eat at a cozy little place, he insists on going where hundreds of his fans can see him. He also brings flowers but asks her to deliver them to another actress at her studio. (Betty, upset, doesn't realize that the other actress is also his sister.) In another strip, Betty finally lures Twinkle over to her house for dinner, even though she can't cook. She hires a female chef who whips up an impressive meal behind the scenes, but then inserts herself as a rival for Twinkle's affections. Despite Van Twinkle's conduct—not to mention his name—he never quite seems to succeed in getting his message across.

CHAPTER 8

Betty seems to have had slightly more luck in an abortive semi-romance with another fellow actor, an upper-class type named Van Scarsdale. (Scarsdale is also the name of an affluent New York City suburb.) The complete background of the Betty-Scarsdale relationship is never told in the comics, except that at one point, apparently after the romance is over, Betty refuses to do a fade-out kiss with him for one of her movies because, she says, she is mad at him. Shortly thereafter, when Betty is required to push a dummy resembling Scarsdale off a cliff in another scene, she "accidentally" lobs the real Scarsdale off the cliff instead. Instead of falling hundreds of feet to his death, Scarsdale is merely shocked and then embarrassed when he falls about ten feet; his coat has caught on a tree branch, saving his life.

In a strip shortly after this incident, Betty, apparently still missing Scarsdale, cheers herself up by soliciting a demonstration of mass affection from her hundreds of male admirers. Her opportunity to do so occurs when her producers tell her they'll have to cut a mob scene from her next picture because it will cost too much. She orders her secretary to call all her male fans and ask them to appear without pay. After the mob has assembled, Betty tosses her garter into the crowd and tells her admirers that whoever brings it back to her can escort her to the premiere of her next picture. This causes an immediate riot. Similarly, when her producers tell her a massive floral display will be needed in her next movie, Betty lets her male fans know she'll be leaving the area for a location shoot the following day. The resulting tide of farewell blossoms stands in for the flower show.

Various other boyfriends make appearances in the strip as well. When her studio balks at renting a mansion for a scene in which Betty has lunch with a millionaire, she has them film an actual lunch she has with a rich man named Jack Darby. When a script calls for pedigreed dogs, she borrows them from the private kennel of another boyfriend, Schuyler Van Gilt. And when the producers want to shoot a scene on a yacht, she asks a third boyfriend, Reggie Van Kush, to lend them his.

Apart from these romantic interests, another new character was Betty's little brother Billy, also known as "Bubby." Except for the first scene in "Minnie the Moocher," in which Betty's father is berating her at the dinner table, the Fleischers had never disclosed anything about Betty's younger years in either her cartoons or her comic strips. That changed with the Sunday full-page strip released on March 10, 1935, in which Bubby made his first appearance. In the strip, Betty has allowed her brother to move in with her in Los Angeles and is doing her best to make him her partner in Hollywood stardom.

(This was a risky decision on Betty's part—not only because Bubby is only seven years old and somewhat of a brat, but because during the 1930s, being a child actor in Hollywood could be dangerous. Around this time, young movie stars Judy Garland and Mickey Rooney routinely worked eighteen-hour days six days a week; after finishing one movie they'd start filming the next one hours later. To keep them going, studio execs would give them amphetamines for energy during the day and sleeping pills at night. And, of course, there was sexual abuse, as would later be recollected by performers like Garland and Shirley Temple.)

After Bubby has passed his first screen test and is called to the studio, Betty insists that he take a bath and comb his hair, hoping he'll impress the executives so much that he'll get a juicy part in a big-budget production. On the way to the studio, as Bubby peppers her with questions about his future, Betty tells him he'll be famous all over the world, his picture will soon be on billboards and in newspapers, and he'll become the male equivalent of Shirley Temple. What Betty hasn't realized is that Bubby's part in the movie, *Ugly Duckling*, is the lead role, which requires him to wear a duck suit covering his entire head and body. For obvious reasons, this sours him on the movie business.

Bubby's resentment, along with his total resistance to doing anything but the absolute minimum required of him by his superiors, persists even after he's inexplicably promoted way above his pay grade by being awarded the lead role in the movie "Little Lord Fauntleroy." To ask Bubby to play this role, the film's director interrupts him while he's playing a baseball game. Bubby angrily throws the blond wig he's supposed to wear for the part right back into the director's face and hurries back to the ballfield to resume the game. In another strip, Bubby is selected to play the lead in the movie "Baby Dumplin.'" When he's wheeled onto the set in a stroller, however, the director makes the mistake of "kitchy-kitchy-kooing" him under the chin as he rolls by. In response, Bubby sticks his finger in the director's eye, thus ending the filming of the scene. Here, as in many of their other strips, the Fleischers were poking their finger in the eye of the industry in a way they rarely could in Betty's cartoons.

9

THE LATER CARTOONS

With Betty's love life rather curtailed in her cartoons during the Code era, much of her attention was redirected to her dog, Pudgy, who became a major focal point of many cartoons. It didn't seem like this would initially be the case. In fact, only four months after dancing with Grampy and friends at Grampy's house, Betty seemed willing to sell Pudgy to a ten-year-old boy named Henry in the cartoon "Betty Boop with Henry, The Funniest Living American," released on December 27, 1935.

Henry was already well-known as a very odd comic strip and cartoon character: a totally bald and usually mute ten-year-old boy who wasn't especially funny and communicated mostly through pantomime (although he'd spoken a few words in some of his early comic strips). To add to the hilarity, he was sometimes drawn without a mouth to emphasis his muteness. The Fleischers were obviously being sarcastic when they called him "The Funniest Living American" in the title of this, Henry's only cartoon with Betty.

Henry approaches the pet store while Pudgy looks on in "Betty Boop with Henry, the Funniest Living American" (1935).

In this cartoon, in the midst of the Great Depression, Betty has somehow found the capital she needs to open a pet store. She is so determined to make the store a success that she works there herself, singing promotional songs such as "Everybody Ought to Have a Pet," a song written specially for this cartoon. Henry wanders in and tells Betty he wants to buy Pudgy for two cents. When she informs him that the price is two *dollars*, he immediately becomes downcast. Betty, moved, then tells Henry he can have Pudgy for nothing if he watches the store for a few minutes while she completes an errand elsewhere. (During the Great Depression, giving a ten-year-old boy a healthy young dog if he'd watch a quiet store for a few minutes arguably indicates that Betty is once again truly conflicted about what she really wants. Does she want to mother and protect Pudgy? Does she want to mother and protect Henry? Or does she want to make money from her store?)

In any case, after leaving the store Betty hands Henry an almost empty box of birdseed, indicating that he should feed it to the store's avian occupants. A few moments later, he heedlessly opens one of the store's large cages and lets all its occupants escape. The birds fly endlessly around the store looking for food, and soon zero in on an open sack of birdseed that Betty has left lying on the floor. Having eaten all the seed in the bag, they then decide to fly out the door and dine on the insects that are crawling on the roof of the building across the street.

As soon as Betty returns from her errand, she tries to recapture the escaped birds by sprinkling birdseed on the sidewalk in front of the store. This fails to attract them, but Henry saves the day by sprinkling birdseed on top of his bald head while he stands in the store's doorway. This somewhat bizarre act, which causes a great many sharp-beaked birds to peck away painfully at his head, works: the pile of goodies he's stacked on his pate attract all the birds, and Betty is then able to recapture them. She gives him the dog as she'd promised, and the situation is resolved.

The Great Depression, which had started in 1929, was still hitting America hard by the middle of the 1930s. Unemployment was endemic, the homeless were a commonplace sight, and the underlying fear this engendered made many Americans bitterly class conscious, a development the Fleischers regularly incorporated into Betty's cartoons. The snobbery of the rich, and the extent to which they'd grown to fear the poor during the 1930s, were nicely demonstrated in "Little Nobody," a Betty Boop cartoon that the Fleischers released the same month as "Betty Boop with Henry."

In this cartoon, Pudgy has grown up to the extent that he is already thinking about romance. After Betty puts him out to play in the yard in front of their small home, he can't help but notice the very glamour-ous female dog with a bow in her hair, relaxing in the luxurious yard of the magnificent home next door. The dog's bow is apparently in imitation of her owner, Mrs. Fritz Ritz, who has accessorized her own hairstyle with a tiara. Before the Depression blighted American social relations, the girl dog might have been interested in Pudgy as a possible boyfriend. After all, why not have a fling, especially when you're a dog? But when Pudgy takes the liberty of approaching her, she demonstrates her contempt for him by literally kicking dirt in his face. Mrs. Fritz Ritz soon adds insult to injury by rushing out into the yard, shooing Pudgy away, and calling him a "Little Nobody." Spurned and insulted, Pudgy begins whimpering as he trudges sadly back into his own yard. Betty, extremely sensitive to her doggie's plight, cradles him in her arms and sings him a song, "Every Little Nobody is Somebody to Someone."

Shortly thereafter Pudgy notices that the beautiful, rich dogette who'd shunned him is riding on a toy merry-go-round that Mrs. Ritz has purchased for her. On this particular doggy-go-round, a tasty treat has been substituted for the traditional gold ring, and the dog who'd snubbed Pudgy finds this morsel so attractive that she lunges ener-getically toward it. Unfortunately, this causes her to fall off and roll down a nearby hill into a rapidly moving river. She soon begins bark-ing desperately for help. At first, remembering how she'd snubbed him, Pudgy walks a few steps in the opposite direction with his nose in the air, obviously tempted to let her drown. However, his hurt feelings are obviously warring with his ingrown desire to be a proud male rescue dog. After hearing more of her whiny screams, he dives in after her. Betty and Mrs. Ritz, drawn to the scene by the barking, encourage Pudgy from the riverbank. With all this encouragement, and with an attractive dogette beckoning him, Pudgy succeeds in rescuing her and becomes her special friend, thus conquering the invidious class distinctions that had separated them in the first place.

In the cartoon "Pudgy Takes a Bow-Wow," released on April 9, 1937, we see Betty applying makeup in her offstage dressing room and then putting Pudgy into his crib for a nap while she performs. (Pudgy, tellingly, is sleeping in a crib and wearing a bonnet and baby clothes.) Once on stage, Betty performs a song in pidgin English, and from her costume and manner, it is clear she is performing an offensive imitation of a Chinese person. She follows this up by slapping on an Italian style mustache and cap and singing a song about an organ grinder, again indulging in ethnic stereotypes. While Betty continues to degrade her fellow Americans in public, a cat awakens Pudgy backstage and challenges him to a fight. As Betty finishes her second song, the fighting between Pudgy and the snarling kitty erupts onto the stage, ending Betty's stream of insulting skits—much to the relief of the majority of modern-day viewers of the cartoon. Luckily for all concerned, the audience bursts into hysterical laughter.

As the 1937–1938 recession—referred to by some as the "recession within the Depression"—eased up, Betty and Pudgy were apparently able to move into a better home. In the cartoon "Pudgy the Watchman," released on August 12, 1938, Pudgy saves Betty from a crooked exterminator who has come to what is clearly a larger and sturdier house. And in the cartoon "The Scared Crows," released on July 19, 1939, we see Betty planting seeds in the garden of a large estate—while wearing high heels, no less. One day, crows begin brazenly digging up and eating Betty's seeds, and neither Betty nor Pudgy can ward off the birds. Finally, they are dispersed when Betty and Pudgy shake a scarecrow at them. But when one crow smashes into a tree and falls to the ground, Betty rushes the unconscious bird into the house and deposits him in Pudgy's cradle to recover. (Yes, Betty is still insisting that Pudgy sleep in a cradle rather than in a dog bed.)

The ungrateful crow then regains consciousness and, noticing that Pudgy is asleep, signals to the other crows that it's safe to enter the house. Once inside, the crows gorge themselves on all the food they can find while easily avoiding Pudgy's pathetic attempts to stop them. Although the marauding birds try to keep poor Pudgy indoors, he manages to bolt out the front door and alert Betty. Now intent on rescuing her household, Betty takes a desperate step: she jumps into the scarecrow's clothes, scaring them off for good.

In the late 1930s the Fleischers introduced another character into Betty's world: Sally Swing, voiced by Rose Marie Mazzetta, known professionally as Rose Marie. Much as Betty had been inspired by Helen Kane, this was an attempt to create another recurring character based on a popular performer—though Sally never appeared in

Betty and Pudgy minister to a hurt bird in "Scared Crows" (1939).

another cartoon. "Sally Swing," released on October 14, 1938, is notable for being one of the few times Betty is shown helping out another woman—in most of her cartoons, her relationships with women are marked by romantic and professional jealousy. In the cartoon, some college students ask Betty to arrange entertainment for their Swing Dance. Two male students volunteer to assist but can't locate any promising entertainers. Left alone with the problem, Betty notices that the lithe, blonde, young cleaning woman who is dusting the outside of her office door at the time is not only humming a swing tune, but dancing along to it. Seeing a solution to her dilemma, Betty gives the cleaning woman the stage name "Sally Swing" and chooses her as the chief entertainer for the party. Backed by skilled student musicians, Sally is a big hit.

Rose Marie, who voiced Sally, was an actress and singer who'd begun performing professionally in 1929 when she was five years old. For over eighty years she worked with some of the same famous people Betty worked with and encountered some of the same problems Betty

"Sally Swing" (1938) marked the only appearance of the title character.

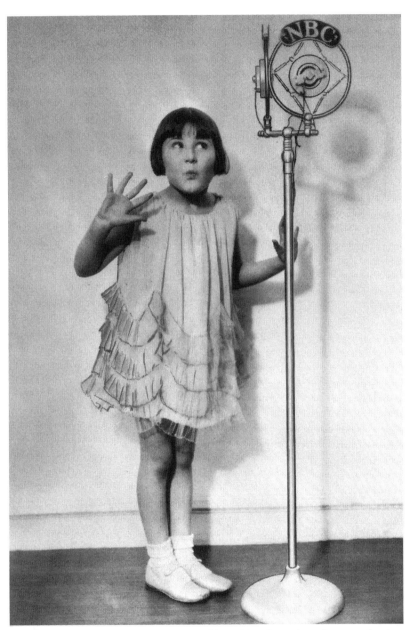

Sally Swing was voiced by Rose Marie Mazzetta, shown here in an early photograph from the June 1930 issue of *What's On the Air*. COURTESY INTERNET ARCHIVE.

faced. African American jazz musicians such as Cab Calloway and Louis Armstrong had accompanied Betty in several of her cartoons. Similarly, Rose Marie's first record, "Say That You Were Teasing Me," a national hit in 1932, featured Fletcher Henderson's band, one of the leading African American jazz orchestras of the day.

Like Betty, Rose Marie appeared in numerous films throughout the 1930s, and continued to appear in them during the 1940s and 1950s. She also provided a dubbed-in voice for Alfred Hitchcock's 1960 movie *Psycho*. Betty and Rose Marie also both later became TV actors, with Rose Marie becoming best known as the character Sally Rogers on *The Dick Van Dyke Show* in the 1960s. She also played Hilda on the police drama *S.W.A.T.* in the mid-1970s, and Frank Fontana's mother on *Murphy Brown* in the 1990s.

Betty and Rose Marie were so much alike that Rose Marie had actually gained attention very early in her career for covering Helen Kane's song "Don't Be Like That," which included a conspicuous "boop-oop-a-doop" scat lyric. On the downside, however, both Betty the cartoon character and Rose Marie the human being sometimes worked for gangsters. According to one of Betty's later animated TV specials, Betty had performed for a while during 1939 at Manhattan's fictional mob-infested Club Bubbles, quitting when the mob took over the club completely. In real life, Rose Marie's father had mob ties, and Rose Marie herself, when she was a child star, as well as during part of her adult career, was chaperoned, managed, and protected by Al Capone, Bugsy Siegel, and company. She was pleased that these men always treated her well, but later complained that they'd skimmed off most of the money she'd earned as a young performer.

CHAPTER 9

Additionally, both Betty and Rose Marie had to fight off sexual predators during their careers. As we've seen, in the 1932 cartoon "Boop-Oop-a-Doop," when Betty was performing on the Big Top high wire early in her animated cartoon career, the grossly overweight ringmaster had made advances on her; with assistance from Koko the Clown, she'd boldly fought him off, retaining her virtue, or what she referred to as her "Boop-Oop-a-Doop." Likewise, Rose Marie would later tell a story about rehearsing the song "I Fought Every Step of the Way" for a scene in the 1954 movie musical *Top Banana*. The song contained several references to boxing, and according to Rose Marie, while she was rehearsing the song she was jabbing and dancing around like a boxer would. When the band stopped in the middle of a lyric, she remarked jokingly, "Don't leave me in a position like this." Everyone laughed, and they all took a five-minute break. During the break, the movie's producer walked over to her and very softly said, "If you're really interested in some good positions, I'd be happy to show them to you."

She laughed and said, "Funny, very funny."

"I mean it," he said. "This could be your picture. I'm the producer and I can see to it that it's your movie, so let me know when you want to learn the new positions."

"Now I knew he wasn't kidding," Rose Marie later wrote. "He meant it. It was the first time anybody had ever made that kind of a pass at me. I was embarrassed and insulted, and then I got very angry, and I mean spittin' mad. In front of the whole crew, singers, dancers, and orchestra, I said loudly, 'Why, you stupid bastard, you couldn't get it up if the flag went by.'"

"Everybody laughed like hell," she wrote. "Then the orchestra started to laugh, and it went like a wave—through the fiddles, saxes, trumpets and trombones." The producer reacted by cutting every one of her musical numbers out of the film.

(To be fair, the parallels between Betty and Rose Marie on the topic of harassment can only be taken so far. A year and a half after "Boop-Oop-a-Doop," Betty allowed her standards to drop considerably. While applying for a job as a secretary, as portrayed in the cartoon "Betty Boop's Big Boss," she sings a song blatantly offering sexual favors to a fat, lusty office supervisor if he'd hire her.)

Betty's last cartoon of the Fleischer era was unfortunate for several reasons. Although the Fleischers had portrayed Native Americans as intelligent and knowledgeable in some of Betty's comic strips, they unfortunately used "Rhythm on the Reservation," released on July 7, 1939, to mock them. The cartoon also portrayed Betty as a half-wit, even though in previous cartoons and most of her comic strips, the Fleischers had portrayed her as sly and intelligent.

As the cartoon begins, Betty is driving along the road on a sunny day in the American West with all the instruments for a swing band piled in the back seat of her roadster. She stops at an Indian reservation gift shop, leaving her car and all its contents unprotected outside the shop. In the shop she buys a Native American drum—the gift store clerk handles the exchange with her in stereotypically pidgin English—while outside, various Indians are stealing all the band instruments, one by one, from her open car.

The cartoon suggests that Native Americans will steal anything they can get their hands on. But it goes further by strongly implying that they have no knowledge whatsoever about what modern European-derived instruments look like or what they could do. Various thieves therefore rush off to use them for numerous purposes for which they

Betty at the opening of her final cartoon of the Fleischer era, "Rhythm on the Reservation" (1939).

hadn't been intended: one uses a tuba to pump water from a ditch into a kettle, another uses a violin as a spark generator to start a fire under a chicken he is roasting, and so on. In real life, anybody would have been incredibly angry at such outright theft and would have moved rapidly to try to prevent damage to the instruments and to take them all back to the car and leave the reservation.

In this cartoon, however, Betty is both pleased and fascinated at the way the Native Americans are manhandling her valuable musical instruments. She then starts singing a swing song while encouraging them to accompany her on the instruments they'd stolen. The song, composed by Fleischer Studios composer Sammy Timberg, included lines such as "Just beat that drum and let it come." After singing "So longum everybody" Betty drives away happily, leaving all her instruments behind.

This is possibly the least realistic Betty Boop cartoon the Fleischers ever produced. Maybe it was appropriate that it was also their last.

By the end of the 1930s, the standards imposed by the Hays Code had made Betty a much less appealing personality in her cartoons than she'd been previously. Not being quitters, however, the Fleischers had kept producing her cartoons without violating the code more than once or twice. They'd also created a host of new characters to join Betty on-screen, including Pudgy, Bubby, and Grampy, and imported more characters from comic strips and animated cartoons produced by others to join Betty in her animated cartoon performances, including Henry. None of that helped much, however.

One of the Fleischers' major problems was that Walt Disney was as energetic, as talented, and as ambitious as they were. In 1937, his studio released the world's first full-length animated feature, *Snow White and the Seven Dwarfs*. It ran for one hour and twenty-three minutes and enabled that studio to vault ahead of the Fleischers forever. (The Fleischer brothers' surrealistic "Snow-White" cartoon had been only seven minutes and seven seconds long.)

Bedeviled by Disney, the Hays Code, and union troubles, the Fleischer brothers had tried to reactivate their mojo in 1938 by moving their operation to Miami. They did so partly on the theory that the cheerful Florida sun, the very same sun that shone down on Disney's headquarters in Burbank, California, would help them compete with him by encouraging their animators to produce more upscale fare. But after Mae Questel, Betty's major voice provider, told the brothers she wouldn't be moving with them, they recalled their recent lack of success with Betty and terminated her Fleischer cartoon career after producing "Rhythm on the Reservation."

The Fleischers' bitterness over losing Betty as a major character and profit producer allegedly inspired the production of an in-house stag cartoon that included an explicit scene showing Popeye assaulting Betty. Although this cartoon was allegedly shown to celebrate their move south, it was, for obvious reasons, never shown in public.

In an attempt to compete with Disney from their new base after sidelining Betty, the Fleischers produced their own full-length cartoon, *Gulliver's Travels*, which they released in 1939. This feature didn't do that well, however, nor did the brothers' next major cartoon effort, *Mr. Bug Goes to Town*. It came out on December 7, 1941, the day the Japanese bombed Pearl Harbor.

Mr. Bug's lack of success ended the Fleischer challenge to Disney. In 1942, the brothers' Hollywood overlord and financial backer, Paramount Pictures, took over the firm, removed the Fleischer brothers from their management positions, moved the company back to New York City and reorganized it as the somewhat less famous "Famous Studios." Considering that Famous Studios was the Fleischer Studio's afterlife, it was appropriate that its most popular character was Casper the Friendly Ghost.

10

BETTY'S COMEBACKS

By this time, Betty had lost some of her corporate sponsors and some of her oomph, but she wasn't done yet. Although she took a long nap starting in 1939, a syndication company acquired her cartoons in 1955 and began showing them regularly on TV stations across the country.

Then, in the 1960s and 1970s, college students unearthed old 16 mm prints of those cartoons to show at campus film festivals across America. This was a key moment in Betty's revival: these students would soon be the middle-class adults of the 1970s–1990s and if they continued to be Betty Boop fans, her commercial future was assured.

Many members of Betty's 1960s and later audiences couldn't help but notice that many of her cartoons were sexier than most of the movies being released at the time. They also took note of cartoons like "Silly Scandals," which originally had been released in 1931 and included a scene in which Bimbo, after being struck on the head, experiences a series of expertly animated hallucinations. The more surreal elements of Betty's cartoons such as this found a particularly interested audience in the 1960s.

CHAPTER 10

In 1974, Betty's fans, now somewhat revved up, launched a touring retrospective film festival titled "Betty Boop's Scandals of 1974." The title was somewhat misleading, because Betty hadn't been involved in any scandals for years, but it showed that the memory of the pre-Code Betty still lingered in the minds of many. Soon thereafter, with the rise of color TV, many of Betty's cartoons were colorized and reshown on broadcast television. Meanwhile, Betty Boop comic books also began appearing in the 1970s. The first one, "Betty Boop Funnies," was released in 1977.

Then, in the late 1970s, encouraged by Betty's resurgent popularity, movie producer Dan Dalton, backed by New Line Cinema, compiled scenes from many of her recently colorized cartoons into a network TV feature, *Betty Boop for President* (also known as *Hurray for Betty Boop*), in which Betty Boop's cartoon character runs for president in 1980.

This was actually not the first time that Betty had run for president. Her first campaign had been made public in the Fleischer cartoon "Betty Boop for President," which was released four days before the election of 1932, on November 4. In that year of economic depression, the incumbent president was Herbert Hoover, a Republican. No one gave Hoover's reelection bid much of a chance. Under his administration the country had fallen from apparent prosperity into the biggest economic depression in its history. In real life, except for the fact that she was a woman, Betty might have had a chance against the unpopular Hoover. Unfortunately, however, Hoover's real opponent was Franklin D. Roosevelt, a popular Democrat who was the governor of New York State.

In any case, in the cartoon, Betty's on-screen presidential campaign is certainly original. At one point she promises to divide all the money in America equally between rich people and poor people. (This is

Cover of the first issue of *Betty Boop Funnies*.

Betty stumps in "Betty Boop for President" (1932).

cleverer than it might appear, because she never explains which Americans she considered rich and which she considered poor.) Very aware of the overwhelming political sentiments of that era, Betty also not only declares herself to be against abortions but goes on to argue grandiloquently in favor of big families. At one point she tells her supporters that if any of them was an only child, she'll struggle to make sure they can have a sibling. Presumably, she plans to do this by making their parents prosperous enough to afford a second kid.

As Betty delivers these promises on stage, her face morphs into caricatures of incumbent Republican president Herbert Hoover and Al Smith, who'd been the Democratic nominee in 1928 and was expected to run again. Because of all the time it took to script, design, and animate the cartoon, it had been created before Roosevelt was nominated but released after he'd been named the Democratic nominee.

In the cartoon, after Betty delivers her routine stump speech, she is quickly succeeded on-screen by her opponent, an anonymous figure creatively dubbed Mr. Nobody. Meant as a caricature of whoever her real-life opponent would be, he tells the crowd that if they are hungry, nobody will feed them; if their spouses leave them, nobody will marry them; and so on. Betty then returns to the on-screen stage to proclaim that under her administration, America will become a "perfect country." She also promises much improved road and rail networks, the creation of weather-interference systems to protect big cities against rainstorms, and the elimination of capital punishment. In fact, she proposes converting the unused electric chairs that will then be available into devices in which convicts are electronically cleaned and buffed up so they can more successfully seek post-prison jobs. Progressive viewers have since criticized the cartoon, however, because the chairs seem to convert the convicts into stereotypes of preening gay men as well as potential job seekers.

Nevertheless, Betty as a presidential candidate is so optimistic about her chances of landing in the White House that she spends time and money planning a personalized inaugural-day parade for herself. Her optimism in this case was of course misplaced, given that in real life Roosevelt won easily. But it seems Betty enjoyed the campaign so much that she was willing to give it another try forty-six years later.

For the 1980 campaign, Victoria D'Orazi provided Betty's voice for her new presidential run and worked diligently to publicize the film. D'Orazi also recorded some of the songs that were used in the film, and Tom Smothers, of the famous Smothers Brothers, voiced Pudgy. Because Smothers had become a politically outspoken leftist, he was an appropriate choice for an allegedly political film.

Cover for the VHS home release of 1980's *Betty Boop for President*, a.k.a. *Hurray for Betty Boop.*

Unfortunately for America First purists, the cartoons had all been colorized in Korea. That could have given rise to charges of foreign interference in an American presidential campaign if Betty had really been running. To add insult to injury, most of the colorization had been done badly, and overall, the feature looked somewhat half-baked.

However, it certainly made sense to portray Betty as a 1980 presidential candidate. She was a former comic strip Hollywood star, and that year Ronald Reagan, a fellow former Hollywood star, was also running for president. That year he was running as a conservative Republican against incumbent Democratic president Jimmy Carter and independent candidate John Anderson.

Dalton, the producer, and many other people, apparently believed that because of the Hollywood heritage Betty shared with Reagan, she'd benefit from all the attention that was being paid to his candidacy. They also noted that because she was younger than Reagan—ageless, in fact—they could present her as an energetic reformist candidate, and Reagan as a tired old man. Deciding that Carter was vulnerable because of his lackluster record, they predicted that Anderson's candidacy would turn the election into a free-for-all, making Betty's on-screen candidacy somewhat plausible.

Noting the pro-business climate of the time, Betty's backers made sure to let the cartoon-watching public know that she had allegedly, and recently, demonstrated her business and organizational acumen by designing a new and popular fashion accessory, a combination stocking/sock for both men and women. (They seemed to ignore the fact that the upper part of the item she'd allegedly designed looked decidedly feminine and that most of her male supporters would be highly unlikely to wear it.) The success of this innovation, however, lets Betty avoid the degrading and time-consuming labor of political fundraising. According to her campaign spokespeople, the stocking/sock has become so successful that she will neither need, nor accept, any campaign donations. Likewise, this would supposedly ensure that she'd never approve legislation or perform any governmental actions at the behest of moneyed interests.

"I will owe no one favors when I become president of the United States," Betty says. To emphasize her freedom from rich political sponsors, she occasionally turns her pockets inside out on stage and reveals that they are empty. Her supporters eat it up: "Betty, Betty, make us all believe again," they sing.

She also makes extraordinary campaign promises. "When I'm president, no one will ever go hungry," she declares. "No one in the United

States, and no one in the entire world." This is difficult to believe, but so are many campaign promises. She adds to it by pledging to give free ice cream to children everywhere, a commitment only slightly less difficult to carry out. Somewhat more mysteriously, Betty also says she'll not only "take care of all the children in every country in the world," but "let them keep their imaginations." Neither of the other candidates have threatened to dampen children's imaginations, so the political effect of this promise is probably limited.

Betty also declares that she'll "preserve all the animals in the forest and make sure that our senior citizens are provided for." One of her campaign videos illustrates the proposed extent of this commitment: it shows that the federal government under her leadership will erect bachelors' halls next to old maid homes throughout America. Naturally, considering what might occur in reaction to the fulfillment of this promise, Betty also says she'll immediately guarantee every US citizen the right to privacy.

While these commitments appeal to numerous voters, Betty's campaign also makes targeted appeals to groups such as Native Americans. In a speech in Phoenix, Arizona, she promises to apologize to them officially once and for all and to "make retribution" for "taking their country." However, Betty's Native American spokesman, the unfortunately named Big Running Mouth, points out to Betty that by teaching white people to smoke tobacco and thus killing millions of them, Native Americans have already evened the score.

As the number of out-of-work Americans had reached 7.5 percent in April 1980, unemployment was another campaign issue. Cartoon candidate Betty promises to put all Americans back to work, but, in a somewhat snarky fictional broadcast, the British Broadcasting Corporation reports that Betty plans to give Americans jobs by encouraging them "to do quality work once again." According to this broadcast, that would mean Americans would manufacture cars that lasted "longer than the installment payments" and also grow and prepare food "that wouldn't poison" the people who ate it.

The cartoon version of the USSR's state radio also chimes in, claiming Betty has pledged to put music in the White House and spread it around the world because it's the only universal language. It also reports that Betty has promised to visit every country in the world and sing and dance for its people as president. Reagan, who was sixty-nine by the time he began his presidential campaign, could hardly make such a promise.

While these vows might attract more votes than they lost, Betty makes two major mistakes as a cartoon presidential candidate. The first one is making Grampy her running mate. This potentially dooms her campaign, as few American presidential candidates, even Donald Trump, have ever shown such blatant favoritism toward a person who may be a blood relative. The second mistake is Betty's assumption, revealed in one of her in-cartoon campaign videos, that poor American whites, or "hillbillies," are completely ignorant not only about how to use gadgets such as waffle irons and outboard motors, but also simple mops, dustpans, and carpet sweepers as well. This insult stinks of urban snobbishness and ignorance, and in real life would have caused Betty no end of grief.

Soon, only the four electors of the State of Hawaii appear to stand between Betty and victory. In an amazing last-minute electoral bid, she dons a grass skirt and a lei that barely conceals her breasts and does a hula dance on a beach in front of the cameras, recycling a scene she'd done in 1932 when flirting with Bimbo in the cartoon "Betty Boop's Bamboo Isle." It was just one of many reused scenes for the special—though oddly, none were taken from her 1932 presidential run.

Due to these creative and original campaign efforts, Betty wins on-screen. If she'd run in reality, she probably would have lost to Reagan; she might even, like her fellow candidate John Anderson, have received zero electoral votes. She'd entranced America, however, and had taken the next step in restoring her popularity as a multimedia character for the rest of the century and beyond.

A few years later, taking note of Betty's renewed popularity, the executives who ran King Features decided to feature her in a comic strip that appeared on both Sundays and weekdays between 1984 and 1988. In this strip, Betty is partnered not with a dog, a dog-man or a human being, but with a cat—Felix the Cat, specifically—who had already appeared in the "Betty Boop Funnies" comic book almost a decade earlier.

Felix had the body of a black cat, and often walked on two legs. If he'd talked, had been nearer Betty's size, and if Betty had fancied him, he might have assumed the same prominence in her life that Bimbo the dog-man had. Felix acted and looked much more like a cat than Bimbo had looked and acted like a dog, however. And Betty gave no indication whatsoever that she was attracted to him romantically.

However, uniting Felix and Betty made sense. Felix had dominated the animated cartoons of the 1920s just as Betty had dominated those of the 1930s, and he'd even beaten her to a major milestone by becoming the first cartoon character who'd been able to attract movie audiences. Unfortunately, Felix's cartoons had all been silent, and his creators hadn't succeeded when they tried to transform him into a speaking cartoon character. Nevertheless, without Betty, Felix had been a comic strip star from 1923 to 1943 and a comic book character from 1948 to 1966. Jazz bands played songs that had been written about him, and his image appeared on numerous items of merchandise. In the 1950s, Felix began appearing in cartoons that were airing on American television, and he later starred in two feature films. His most famous incarnation, with his hands behind his back and his head down, deep in thought, became a major trademark.

King Features hired Brian, Morgan, Neil, and Greg Walker, the sons of Mort Walker, who'd created the *Beetle Bailey* comic strip, to draw a strip that featured both Betty and Felix. First titled *Betty Boop and Felix*, it was later dubbed *Betty Boop and Friends*. The somewhat odd, but creative, idea behind the new strip was that Betty and Felix live together in an apartment as a working actress and a retired superstar cat while spoofing the rich and famous personalities of the entertainment world. Betty *talks* in real words that appear in bubbles over her head, and Felix *thinks* in real words that appear over his head.

Greg Walker told an interviewer in 1984 that he and his brothers featured Felix in the strip as a celebrity in his own right. They also avoided making him too much like a cat. "He's very independent but realizes a good deal when he sees it," Greg said, referring to Betty's willingness to keep him as a pet. Although Felix doesn't have much to do in the strip, Betty is portrayed as hardworking: she's out every day doing modeling assignments, practicing her lines for a play, or appearing at various locations for films. She is often frustrated with the roles she gets, hates not getting the credit or recognition she thinks she deserves, and doesn't like performing in what she sees as demeaning commercials. Meanwhile, Felix stays at home most of the time watching TV or playing video games with his friends.

The other celebrities and "beautiful people" included in the strip are based on real people using their real names or stage names. They often visit Betty because she is one of them: a film star. Betty enjoys hosting them, but Felix isn't all that impressed. Also adding tension to the strip is an adversarial relationship between Betty and Felix on one side and Betty's agent on the other: Betty and Felix both blame the agent for not getting Betty the serious acting roles she desires.

The quality of the humor in the strip varies considerably. In a 1984 full-page Sunday strip, Betty and an unnamed starlet are at the beach. The starlet is wearing a very small bikini as she frantically points out that actors John Travolta, Sylvester Stallone, and Tom Selleck are only a few feet away. When Betty suggests that the two of them go for a swim, the starlet says, "OK, but I have to go put on my bathing suit." When Betty asks, "Isn't that a bathing suit you have on?" the starlet says, "Gosh, no! This is my baiting suit!"

The two- or three-frame daily strips were similar but not over-whelming. In one 1984 daily strip, Betty and another woman are walk-ing on the sidewalk with Felix when Betty tells him, "Felix! Don't be so sadistic!"

"What's he doing?" the other woman asks. "Crossing people's paths on purpose," Betty responds.

Some of the strips try to penetrate the culture of Hollywood and occasionally seem to provide some insights. In a 1985 Sunday strip, a film director and Betty are walking around a Hollywood movie set when the director tells her, "We had to settle for Ron Howard as the director on this film," and Betty replies, "Oh, he's just super!" In the next frame, the director complains that "The studio wants Randy

Newman to do the score," and Betty replies "I just love his music!" This goes on for a while until the director says, "Listen, Betty, this is Hollywood. If you can't say something nasty about someone, don't say anything at all!"

The strips also feature some nice interpersonal humor. In a 1985 daily strip, Betty's mustachioed boyfriend Swavo asks her to marry him, and she replies "I don't think so. Why can't we just be good friends?" Felix is shown to be thinking, "Because good friends don't share bank accounts." In a 1988 daily strip, when Swavo asks Betty if he can borrow some money, she asks him "What happened to the $500 I loaned you yesterday?" He replied "I spent $200 at the track, $100 for a massage, $150 for partying last night. . . . And the rest I squandered foolishly."

Sometimes Felix himself also managed to hit a funny bone. In one 1985 strip, Betty is told she has to leave her apartment immediately to make it on time to an appointment and complains in response that

Panel from the 1980s comic strip "Betty Boop and Felix," showing Felix as well as Betty's boyfriend Swavo.

she'll have to cancel her voice lesson to do so. Felix, who'll have to accompany her, thinks, "Hmph! Big deal. I have to miss a golf date with Garfield, Morris, and Heathcliff."

And sometimes celebrities are mildly and humorously teased: In a 1985 Sunday strip, Betty goes jogging while Felix calls it a waste of time and compares it unfavorably to smoking and drinking. He then mentions that he developed this belief after reading the (fictional) *Dean Martin's Exercise Book*.

A major problem for Betty Boop fans reading this strip was that it portrayed Betty not as the seductive siren, the aggressive manhunter, the queen of surrealism, or the sly comedian she'd previously been portrayed as, but as a rational young woman with a mildly sarcastic cat. Many readers seem to have found this somewhat boring. The strip appeared in about one hundred newspapers at its peak but failed to catch on and was canceled in 1988. At least it went out with a reference to Betty's previous fabulous on-screen history. The final Sunday strip, dated January 31, 1988, shows Betty on stage at a Fleischer Studio reunion saying, "Thank you folks. . . . Good-Bye!" and then discussing her old friends. She calls Bimbo her first boyfriend, Pudgy her loyal pup and goes on to note that when she needed a laugh, Koko was always there. She also says people could always count on Grampy for good advice, and that "Uncle" Max Fleischer, who is identified in the strip as the creator of the "Out of the Inkwell" cartoon series (an early Fleischer production in which Betty first appeared), had aided her when she was first starting out. Betty says Max taught her everything she knows and that when her agent asks her where he is now, she responds, "Back in the inkwell, I guess." This may have been true, but Betty hadn't accompanied him there.

The story of the 1985 TV special *The Romance of Betty Boop* was set in 1939.

While Betty and Felix were appearing in their daily and Sunday comic strip, another animated Betty Boop TV special, a half-hour-long colorized cartoon titled *The Romance of Betty Boop*, was broadcast on network television in 1985 and 1987. The cartoon is set in 1939, with Betty selling shoes during the day and singing at a nightclub in the evening. In the cartoon, her attempt to marry a rich man results in her rescue by Freddy, whom she then leaves behind to move to Hollywood and become a comic strip movie star.

Lee Mendelson, one of the cartoon's producers, called Betty "a good representative of the women's movement today." He added that Betty "wants to settle down but she wants a career, too. She's a female paradox." That last remark, which he made in the mid-1980s, indicated that Mendelson may have been somewhat behind the times.

In the film, Betty changes her outfit several times and has a pet parrot called Polly, who seems to have replaced Pudgy, Betty's pet pooch. Oddly, Betty doesn't wear her garter belt throughout the whole cartoon even though the Hays Code rules were long gone by then and the garter had been one of Betty's trademarks in her earlier cartoons.

This cartoon also marked the first time that Betty had sung Helen Kane's signature song, "I Wanna Be Loved By You," and made it her own. The film's producers had undoubtedly been attracted to the song by Marilyn Monroe's sultry rendition of the tune in her 1959 hit movie *Some Like It Hot* when they decided to add it to the video presentation.

In another attempt to bring Betty up to date for this film, her backers provided her with a new voicer, Desiree Goyette. Then twenty-nine, Goyette, a graduate of the San Francisco Conservatory of Music, was certainly qualified for the job because of her skill, education, and experience. It would be difficult to believe, however, that her marriages hadn't helped her somewhat: her second husband was Lee Mendelson, one of the producers of this video, and her third husband was Ed Bogas, who'd composed its score. Goyette also had voiced several songs and characters on the first three seasons of the TV show *Garfield and Friends*, and later recorded several inspirational albums. She also wrote three original songs that Betty sings in the cartoon, much as she had done for *Garfield and Friends* and for several *Peanuts* specials.

In *The Romance of Betty Boop*, Betty and her environment have been somewhat modernized. Her accent has been toned down, and she is selling women's shoes at a Manhattan department store while moonlighting as a singer at Club Bubbles, her uncle's nightclub. Freddy, her fully human boyfriend, works as an iceman during the day, and attends law school classes at night. Hopelessly in love with Betty, he sings the song "I Only Have Ice for You" in a duet with Betty just before she gets a phone call from Hollywood and leaves Freddy behind to begin her career out west.

The other characters in the cartoon included a parrot who end-lessly repeats President Franklin Roosevelt's speeches, a villain named Johnny Throat, and a millionaire playboy, Waldo Van Lavish. When Betty asks, "Tell me about the market. I have one share of United Pea-nut Butter. What should I do?" Van Lavish replies, "Merge it with Con-solidated Jelly."

Those who'd invested their money, time, and creativity in Betty's ongoing rebirth were very pleased only a short while later when she landed a small but highly lauded part in the massively successful movie *Who Framed Roger Rabbit*, released on June 22, 1988. Especially pleased was Mae Questel, who provided Betty with a voice in this movie fifty-seven years after she'd first done so in 1931. Betty's garter also reap-peared in *Rabbit*, thus emphasizing the fact that she was legging it back toward cinematic glory once again.

Critics loved *Rabbit*, which became the second-highest-grossing movie of the year, just behind *Rain Man*, starring Dustin Hoffman. It ultimately won three Academy Awards: for Best Film Editing, Best Sound Effect Editing, and Best Visual Effects, plus a Special Achieve-ment Academy Award for animation. And in 2016, the Library of Con-gress selected it for the United States National Film Registry, calling it "culturally, historically, or aesthetically significant." Ironically, consid-ering the long competition that had taken place between the Fleisch-ers, Betty's creators, and Walt Disney, the Fleischers' major opponent, *Rabbit* was jointly created by the Walt Disney studios working with Amblin entertainment and included the Fleischers' most successful cre-ation, Betty.

Reviewers and audiences in general were astounded by the fluid on-screen mix between the movie's animated characters and its real-life actors. The movie is a vivid and colorful one, but apparently in honor of her classic cartoons, which were all in black and white, Betty is the only cartoon star in the film who is presented in that way rather than in color. When Betty appears in the film as a cigarette girl, she calls out "Cigars? Cigarettes?" while strolling among the diners and drinkers in the fictional Ink & Paint Club. This modest role was certainly a comedown from her nightclub appearance in her very first cartoon, "Dizzy Dishes," in which she'd played an on-stage female vocalist.

Betty's appearance comes about seventeen minutes into the movie, which is set in Hollywood in 1947. Its human hero, Eddie Valiant, a private eye played by actor Bob Hoskins, is having a drink in the Club. The plot of the movie revolves around Valiant, who's been hired by Roger Rabbit to discover if Marvin Acme, head of the Acme Corporation, and his wife Jessica have been fooling around, or, as the film puts it, "playing patty-cake." (In one scene, Acme and Jessica actually play patty-cake. The movie is a comedy, after all.) When Acme is murdered, Roger Rabbit becomes the prime murder suspect, but as the movie's title proclaims, he's been framed.

Valiant sees and greets Betty, who replies, "Long time no see!" He asks her what she's doing working in the club, rather than on screen, and she tells him, "Work's been kinda slow since cartoons went to color, but I still got it, Eddie, Boop-Oopy-Doop-Boop!"

Valiant agrees that she still has it, but then asks about Marvin Acme, who is sitting nearby spraying himself with perfume. Meanwhile, Jessica Rabbit has begun to perform on stage. Betty tells Detective Valiant that Acme never misses a night when Jessica is performing. "[He's] got a thing for rabbits, huh?" Valiant says to Betty. When Jessica appears on stage, Betty pulls up her garter, which has worked its way down her

Betty's was one of the more memorable cameos in *Who Framed Roger Rabbit* (1988). Here she flirts with Bob Hoskins's Eddie Valiant in the movie's Ink & Paint Club.

left leg.

Jessica, an overwhelming and underdressed human (but animated) female sexpot with a battleship chest, then begins singing and slinking around the stage as every man in the audience, including Valiant, watches her open-mouthed. (Actress Kathleen Turner, who was heavily pregnant at the time, provided Jessica with her very sultry voice.) When Jessica stops singing, Betty reaches over and closes Valiant's mouth, which is still hanging open.

"*She's* married to Roger Rabbit?" Eddie asked Betty incredulously. "Yeah," Betty replies, and adds "What a lucky goil!" Although in the film Jessica is obviously human, her husband Roger looks like a normal cartoon rabbit, wearing overalls and a bow tie. He also has a thatch of red hair sticking out of his skull that exactly matches the color of Jessica's luxurious mane.

The movie's Ink & Paint Club looks like the jazz clubs in Harlem that had heavily influenced the development of Betty's character. The resemblance becomes more meaningful when, over the course of the movie, the audience learns that the human patrons in the Ink & Paint club are first-class citizens while the cartoon characters, who are always called "Toons," are second-class folks forbidden to sit at the tables or visit the club as patrons. In the Harlem clubs where two of Betty's prototypes, Little Esther and Baby Esther, had performed and white patrons were welcome, black performers were forbidden to sit at tables or otherwise patronize these places. The name of the club in the film, "Ink & Paint," an obvious take off on the idea of a "color line," emphasizes the similarity of the two situations, as does the fact that the Toons live in a ghetto called "Toon Town," and that a movie within the movie is being produced by the Maroon Cartoon company. These parallels sprang from the mind of Gary K. Wolf, the author of the book on which the film is based, *Who Censored Roger Rabbit?*

Actor Charles Fleischer, who provided Roger Rabbit's voice, would have linked Betty and her predecessor even closer to the film's story line if he'd been related to the Fleischers who ran Fleischer Studios. There's no evidence that he was, however.

The attention paid to Betty's role in the film surprised many critics, considering that she is on-screen for less than two minutes total and appears in black and white while all the other characters are presented in full color. One possible reason for the seemingly exaggerated public interest in Betty's performance in the film became clearer when the movie was released in March 1994 on the now-obsolete LaserDisc video format. Alert watchers discovered several scenes in the film in which Betty misbehaved in ways reminiscent of her earlier career. While the scenes were undetectable when the LaserDisc version of the film was played at the usual rate of twenty-four frames per second, they became visible when fanatic Boop fans viewed the movie frame-by-frame. These fans had discovered that in some versions of the film, in one crowd scene, Betty repeats her old trick of dropping the top of her dress to reveal her cleavage. In other versions, when Bugs Bunny and Betty are running alongside each other, Bugs is moving his carrot close to Betty's groin. Many retailers said they'd sold out their entire stock of LaserDisc versions of the film within minutes after the rumors about Betty's nudity began circulating.

Betty's popularity was obviously undimmed, and her fans harbored high hopes that her well-publicized role in a hit picture like *Who Framed Roger Rabbit* would once again loft her to the top of the Hollywood acting pyramid. Unfortunately, her coactor Jessica Rabbit's sex appeal and acting skill, to say nothing of her major role in the movie compared to Betty's, eclipsed Betty's contribution. Betty would try to succeed again, however, by appearing in the animated TV special *The Betty Boop Movie Mystery*, also known as *Betty Boop's Hollywood Mystery*, in 1989, in which she played the role of a waitress who solves a Hollywood murder.

By 1990, Betty had been pushing the boundaries of proper sexual conduct for years. As we've seen, she'd started off her Fleischer cartoon career by vigorously wooing Bimbo, a dog-man, as well as several fully human men, and to do so, she'd worn short skirts and abbreviated tops. Also, on several occasions she'd allowed parts of whatever outfit she was wearing to blow upward or drop downward. Then, during her career as a Hollywood comic strip star, she'd been so persistent in her pursuit of men, and so blinded by this persistence, that she'd spent a significant amount of time and effort trying to woo a gay man who kept signaling to her that he wasn't interested in women.

All of this is important background for her 1990 comic book *Betty Boop's Big Break*, which contains a remarkable amount of sexual innuendo even by the standards set by Betty's career. The comic tells the story of Betty's adventures at the Coney Island Amusement Park in the summer of 1990. Her job there requires her to sing and dance in front of the Tunnel of Love and lure visitors inside. (An underclothed woman dancing at the entrance to a love tunnel is an obvious sexual come-on.) Accompanying her at the tunnel entrance is Bimbo, whose job, appropriately enough, is to stand nearby, guide the boats into the tunnel, and prevent them from colliding with each other.

Bimbo had mentioned to her earlier that Koko, now a movie director, is heading up a small movie crew that will be shooting one-reel shorts at the park that day. Betty immediately sees this as a chance for exposure that might put her back in Hollywood again, or at least give her an excuse for having a good time. When Bimbo and Betty reach the park, however, they are confronted by Grampy, who is now a Coney Island maintenance worker. He insists that they help him repair the park's biggest attraction, the renowned Coney Island Cyclone roller coaster.

The two of them are about to start helping Grampy when their boss, who is nearby, announces that they've arrived thirty-seven seconds after their starting time. As a result, he says, he'll not only dock them one hour's pay, but require them to work during their lunch hour that day without extra pay. Fearful of losing her job, or any more of her income, Betty immediately runs to her dressing room and changes from street clothes into the costume she is required to wear while working.

By this point, however, Bimbo has apparently begun to imagine that Betty, who had abandoned him for Freddy and others more than

Cover of the 1990 comic book *Betty Boop's Big Break*.

fifty years previously, is romantically interested in him. So he says with a smile that he wants to "help" her change into her costume. She immediately shoos him away, however.

Soon after the two of them have begun working, Betty notices that Grampy has somehow not only rerouted the tunnel-of-love boats but also the stream on which they floated, onto the roller coaster. Visitors to the tunnel, who'd undoubtedly been looking forward to a romantic cruise in the dark, are startled when they suddenly find themselves hurtling down a raging river on a roller coaster in broad daylight.

Betty's boss, assuming that Grampy's mistake is all Betty's fault, is soon screaming at her. His anger only increases when the water overflow from the tunnel floods much of the park a short while later. However, the water also propels Betty and Bimbo toward Koko and his film crew. Koko, happy to have actors delivered to him by accident—and, even better, actors he knows—immediately provides Betty with a lion costume. He says he wants to star her in a short jungle epic that will use the Coney Island Jungle Ride as a backdrop.

Meanwhile, Bimbo, still driven by his renewed interest in Betty, once again begins spying on her while she tries to change into the tight new full-length lion costume Koko has given her. But Koko gives Bimbo a white hunter's outfit and tells him the script requires him to capture "the big pussy cat"—that is, Betty. At this point Betty's excitement markedly increases. "Oh Bimbo, you can tame me anytime!" she purrs. Koko, now playing Tarzan and wearing a tiger skin, swings onto the set on a vine.

Now pursued by two prospective lovers, Betty appears totally overcome. She flings herself on Koko, saying "Oh Koko, you're too much for me! I surrender! Purrrrrrrrr . . ." Bimbo, as directed by Koko, then strikes Betty several times on the back with his whip. When she responds by threatening to strike him, he says "Heh-Heh! I love it when they get rough!"

The implied and actual bondage scenarios continue for much of the rest of the comic, with Betty's lion tail tied to a tree followed by Betty's confinement in a mummy costume, pursued at various points by Koko, Bimbo, Grampy, Freddy—who makes a surprise appearance—and the

Bimbo, Koko, and other familiar characters made appearances in *Betty Boop's Big Break*.

throngs of other male attendees at the park. Outside of the unsanctioned co-opting of Betty in, say, the "Tijuana Bibles" of the 1930s or the hidden frames of *Who Framed Roger Rabbit*, the entire comic is one of the most erotically charged narratives in which she has appeared—a mix of the sensibility of her earliest cartoons with the much different cultural landscape that was emerging at the end of the twentieth century.

11

BETTY TODAY

Although Betty Boop's one hundredth year of existence is rapidly approaching, she remains extremely popular, especially with women. After all, she's the first woman ever portrayed in cartoons who isn't linked to a man as a wife or long-term girlfriend. She has a career, romance, and fun, but never lets one aspect of her life eclipse any of the others. While romantically interested in various males, she never ties the knot with any of them. Instead, on several occasions, she has refused their advances so she could continue to pursue her cartoon, comic strip, comic book, radio, television, video, and movie career.

Also, while innocent-looking and wide-eyed, Betty's clearly intelligent. She stays independent and often gets what she wants. As one of her female fans told an interviewer, "Betty is a free spirit. While asserting herself, she remains feminine." She also has made herself an archetype of the changing role of women in modern American life. As she aptly put it in her cartoon, "Betty Runs for President," "I'm going to prove a woman can do anything a man can do."

CHAPTER 11

In almost any situation, Betty can choose to play the role of a traditional American woman, a traditional American man, or a mixture of both. She's made it very clear that throughout her career, the choice in any given situation is always going to be hers, and no one else's.

This has all played a part in her enduring popularity. She was the most popular balloon at the Macy's Thanksgiving Day Parade for several recent years. Her Facebook page has 1.4 million followers. She's ubiquitous on YouTube, where all her Fleischer Studios cartoons may be viewed in their entirety and without charge; the copyright on all of Betty's classic cartoons, which were released from 1930 to 1939, expired in 2019.

Several full-length comic books have recently appeared detailing Betty's latest adventures. Several full-length video documentaries and other productions highlighting various aspects of her life have also shown up on television and the internet in recent years. Movies, TV specials and stage plays starring her are being prepared. She has, in fact, become a major American icon.

As a result, more than 100,000 separate Betty Boop products are being marketed to her millions of mostly female fans, indicating a seemingly insatiable need for Betty Boop items. Many American women, and some men, have reacted enthusiastically to Betty's life story by becoming major collectors of Boop memorabilia.

Manufacturers worldwide have produced millions of Betty Boop items over the past ninety-three years. These manufacturers were encouraged by a 2011 ruling by the United States Court of Appeals for the Ninth Circuit. The ruling upheld a lower court's decision that a half-dozen manufacturers of Betty Boop merchandise hadn't infringed on Fleischer Studios' copyright because the new corporate owners couldn't demonstrate that there was one.

The flood of products began as early as 1934 with wooden Betty Boop dolls and the Betty Boop Pocket Watch. Today, more than 2,000 different Betty Boop products are available on Amazon, along with 9,000 on Etsy, an amazing 67,000 on eBay, and hundreds more on a variety of other sites. More than $1 billion worth of Betty Boop goods are sold every year.

Her image has been used on all sorts of merchandise, including pocketbooks, coats, tea sets, cards, Big Little Books, dolls, watches, sweatshirts, bathing suits, sweaters, napkins, cigarette cases, scarfs, scarf pins, nail polish, school tablets, tea sets, buttons, radio sets, marbles, playing cards, candy, dancing dolls, toy racing cars, perfumed soap, and handkerchiefs.

Other Betty Boop products for sale include socks, slippers, purses, mugs, sweaters, T-shirts, dolls, jewelry, lamps, sun glasses, makeup kits, chimes, necklaces, sweatshirts, housekeys, watches, blankets, coin purses, model cars, tote bags, bedspreads, greeting cards, ceramics, wine bottles, seat covers, thongs, jigsaw puzzles, clocks, water bottles, radios, workout shorts, carpets, dolls, license plate frames, salt-and-pepper shakers, onesies, key rings, cell phone cases, bobblehead dolls, flasks, decorative license plates, suitcases, makeup bags, cremation urns, toilet seat covers, backpacks, coffee cups, decals, soap bars, candies, tea sets, checks, lingerie and room deodorizers. Residents of the United States, France, and Brazil have been among the items' major purchasers.

So many Betty Boop collectibles have appeared that their buyers have been trying, and failing for years, to organize their collections by date of production. Thousands of collectors were happily surprised a few years ago when they realized that their early Betty Boop dolls had sixteen knobs or curls on their heads, while those that were produced later on sported only ten. This made it much easier to index the thousands of dolls in hundreds of private collections.

Betty's popularity also has extended itself into the natural world. Among four new flowers that were recognized as All-America Roses in 1999 was the "Betty Boop," an ivory-yellow floribunda with a red edge. According to the official citation, "The natural growth habit of the Betty Boop is rounded with a height of about four feet," meaning that the rose is not much shorter than Betty herself. Several racehorses and racing dogs have been named partly or fully after Betty, including a 2001 racing dog named Abdo Betty Boop.

Meanwhile, numerous nations, including Chad, Gambia, Mongolia, Guinea, Granada, and Mozambique, have latched on to the Boop phenomenon by issuing postage stamps in her honor. In 1999, for instance, the government of Mozambique issued a set of nine oversized stamps that it said "captured the essence of Betty Boop—curvaceous, flirtatious, and a little bit wild." Seven of the stamps showed Betty riding or posing behind a motorcycle, and one showed the curvaceous Ms. Boop thumbing a ride while wearing a short skirt with fishnet stockings and toting a presumably empty gas can.

The Betty Boop franchise has grown into a global marketing phenomenon. During the latter half of the twentieth century, Betty appeared in promotions for Lancôme, Benetton, Adidas, Mastercard, Coca-Cola, NASCAR, Harley-Davidson, and Universal Theme Parks. No mere commercial or national promotion, however, can explain the extent of the Boop memorabilia boom.

Some men and women who purchased large numbers of Betty Boop items were motivated to do so after being traumatized by events such as contracting fatal illnesses or learning of the deaths of close relatives.

Mozambique was one of several countries to issue stamps featuring Betty.

This forced them to reevaluate their own stance toward life and admire Betty's apparent immortality. For instance, Linda McGregor of Kellner, Wisconsin, began her Boop collection after she'd been diagnosed with non-Hodgkin's lymphoma in 2003. By 2011, she owned a Betty Boop shower curtain, a Betty Boop straw wreath, and numerous Betty Boop pictures, blankets, movies, dresses, bobblehead dolls, cell-phone charms, and lunchboxes.

Jessica Varga, of New Carlisle, Indiana, started buying Boop memorabilia after a beloved aunt, whose first name was Betty, had passed down her own collection to Varga. By 2002, an entire room in Varga's home was filled with Betty Boop collectibles, including Betty Boop cups, calendars, pictures, posters, and pins. For a while, Varga was even thinking about purchasing a Betty Boop toilet seat at Walmart that she could add to her aunt's passed-down collection. Her husband objected, however, telling her that "No way I'm peeing on Betty Boop."

Gary Kinney of Des Moines, a US Postal Service mail handler, started his collection as a tribute to his late aunt, Betty Bowlby. Possibly prompted by the fact that she and Betty Boop had the same initials, he was a major Betty Boop admirer. Kinney said in 2001 that he'd spent $30,000 on Boop collectibles during the previous three years. The pride of Kinney's collection of more than one thousand Boop items is one of the largest Boop pieces ever manufactured: a six-foot, six-inch hard resin statue that cost him $1,025 and was shipped to him from Hollywood, Florida. In its protective packaging, the statue was so large that when it arrived, he had to unpack it on his lawn before moving it into his living room. It's the first thing visible on entering his house. Kinney's brother, aware of his enthusiasm for all things Boop, gave him a Betty Boop tambourine decorated with flowing ribbons, and Kinney's seventy-two-year-old mother showed her approval of his efforts by decorating her ankle with a Betty Boop tattoo.

The top floor of Kinney's split-level home, which includes three bedrooms, two baths, and a hallway, is covered with Betty Boop objects. Nevertheless, he said he was planning to expand his collection into the living room. Among his possessions are a Betty Boop waffle maker, a Betty Boop lava lamp, twenty-one Boop cookie jars, fifty Boop water globes, forty Boop coffee mugs, and thirteen lunch boxes. He's hoping he'll eventually be able to afford a Betty Boop jukebox priced at $6,999. Happy with his hobby, Kinney noted fondly that the clerks behind the counter in local memorabilia stores smile broadly each time he enters.

Nancy Springstead, a circuit court clerk who lives in Hart, Michigan, started collecting Boop memorabilia in 1986, a few days after someone had given her a Betty Boop toy bank. Interviewed ten years later, Springstead said that Betty "was so cute, I just couldn't stop." She has searched out Boop memorabilia as far west as Las Vegas and in numerous nearer towns and cities and her home is so overrun with Boop memorabilia that her husband has joked about adding a room to the house to accommodate the expanding collection.

Springstead's Boop possessions include clocks, glasses, checks, playing cards, trading cards, calendars, a miniature tea set, a lamp, music boxes, a mailbox, plates, address labels, picture frames, purses, teapots, wall hangings, figurines, blankets, wrapping paper, golf balls, rugs, pens, earrings, and perfumes. They have overflowed her house and now occupy her office and car as well. She has no idea how many Boop items she's accumulated but insists that Betty was the first and last figure to inspire her to collect so compulsively. In fact, before becoming a Boopist, she'd never collected anything. Now, when people ask her why she's collected so much Boop memorabilia, she has a stock answer. "I don't know," she says. Perhaps Springstead is embarrassed to tell others how much she appreciates Betty.

Molly Dougan, another Betty fan who's a factory worker in Dunkirk, Indiana, rises in the morning, pulls back her Betty Boop bedspread, steps into her bathroom through her Betty Boop hanging beads, and observes herself in her Betty Boop mirror. Often wearing her Betty Boop pajamas, bathrobe, and slippers, she admires her Betty Boop shower curtain, Betty Boop bath mat, Betty Boop soap-on-a-rope, Betty Boop bubble bath, Betty Boop washcloth, Betty Boop towels, Betty Boop hair dryer, and Betty Boop cotton-ball holder. When it's time to get dressed, Dougan puts on her Betty Boop thong underwear, her Betty Boop T-shirt, her Betty Boop sweatshirt, and her Betty Boop jeans or combines bib overalls with her Betty Boop leather jacket. Dougan figures she has about nine thousand Betty Boop items in her house, where a "Betty Boop Way" sign hangs over her garage door.

After entering her home, Dougan checks her email on her computer while peering through her Betty Boop screen saver and sitting in her Betty Boop chair. She and her husband, a retired truck driver, have traveled as far north as Canada and as far south as Florida to purchase Betty Boop memorabilia from antique stores and flea markets. They also buy numerous Boop items online. Dougan's forty-inch-tall Betty Boop bedroom lamps, and her Betty Boop whiskey dispenser, help her read and relax at night.

"Betty Boop makes you feel like you can do anything you want, be anything you want," Dougan says. She added that her Betty Boop memorabilia reminds her of her mom, the late Martha Lacey. "Mom could change a flat tire on a car and cook an elegant meal, all in one day," she said. "She was a survivor, just like Betty Boop and me."

Today Betty does not just live on in memorabilia, however. She was arguably never a bigger star, or rose higher in the sky, than she did during the annual Macy's Thanksgiving Day Parades in New York City starting in 1986. At her first appearance at the parade, which runs from 77th St. in Manhattan to Macy's 34th Street flagship store, Betty became only the second female cartoon character to ever grace the event. (Olive Oyl, Popeye's girlfriend, had taken part in the parade on three prior Thanksgivings.)

Betty's importance to pop character ballooning may be judged from the fact that while most pop figures are allowed to participate in Macy's Thanksgiving Parade on only three occasions, Betty has so far participated in six.

Betty's gains in dimension on behalf of Macy's were astounding. From her usual petite feminine figure, she expanded to a height of seventy-two feet, voluptuous vital statistics of thirty-four by twenty-four by thirty-six feet, and a weight of 425 pounds.

Betty underwent this major transformation by ingesting a good deal of noxious gas so she could float slowly from upper Manhattan to Macy's flagship store at Herald Square while millions of fans watched in person or on TV on Thanksgiving Day. It must be noted that Betty had achieved her enormous gain in height, bulk, and weight without sacrificing one ounce of her beauty.

In that 1986 parade, her first, Betty wore a bright red top hat, white shirt, black buttoned-up vest, and red jacket, along with short shorts ending just above a white garter strap. Many people watching the parade were so excited by her presence and appearance that they chanted "Boop-boop-a-doop" as she neared, and while she preened in front of them. They continued to chant after she was gone.

Betty Boop Balloon in the 1986 Macy's Thanksgiving Day Parade in New York City. PHOTOGRAPH BY JOE SOHM/VISIONS OF AMERICA/UNIVERSAL IMAGES GROUP VIA GETTY IMAGES.

Due to the hundreds of pounds that she'd recently acquired, Betty participated in that event while sitting on a bright yellow balloon shaped like a half-moon. Considering that the parade was scheduled to take three hours to move forty-four blocks, sitting was definitely a good idea; the other ninety-eight balloon characters had to float the whole way standing up. While resting on her half-moon platform, Betty attracted thunderous applause from the alleged three million people in the crowd and no doubt unheard gasps from the alleged fifty million additional spectators who were watching on television.

Unfortunately, those responsible for Betty's physical well-being prior to this, her first appearance at the parade, had failed to prepare her properly for the gale-force winds that struck the parade without warning that year. The wind, combined with the height at which Betty was floating, made her trip down the avenue a tad risky. A trouper if there ever was one, for a while it seemed that she'd be able to persevere. But the wind soon managed to rip the half-crescent moon right out from under her, and with nowhere to sit, she had to be carried straight home.

Some other cartoon-character balloons in the previous year's parade had fared even worse. Superman and Olive Oyl, for instance, hadn't even been able to get airborne, one of Woody Woodpecker's legs had fallen off, and Raggedy Ann had smashed into a streetlight. Kermit the Frog had actually crossed the finish line, but he'd been draped on the shoulders of his handlers by then.

Ironically, Betty's grounding, and the resultant publicity, may have increased her popularity. Although the average balloon was limited by Macy's protocols to one three-year term as a member of the parade, Betty was invited to float down to 34th Street again whenever she wished, and did so without incident in the 1987, 1991, 1992, 1995, and 1996 parades.

Betty has also been the subject of at least two self-help books aimed at contemporary young women. After all, Betty's popularity has grown and her relevance to the lives of women has expanded partly because modern women appreciate the fact that she knew the sort of man she wanted and went after him while successfully defending herself against sexual harassers. They also saw that although she herself was never tied down by marriage or children, she has nevertheless treated kids well. Millions of women also couldn't help noticing that Betty also had managed to hold numerous jobs and obviously knew how to take care of herself both mentally and physically.

In *How to Be a Betty: The Ultimate Guide to Unleashing Your Inner Boop!*, published by Ballantine Books in 2005, the book's author, Sherrie Krantz, lauds Betty in almost every possible way. She credits Betty, or "Ms. Boop," as she calls her, with "a quiet self-confidence, a smile that radiates, and a healthy dose of sex appeal." She also lauds Betty for her ability "to handle any and every situation that's thrown her way" and insists that Betty "is a woman who will find true love and . . . can break any glass ceiling."

Having established Betty as a role model, Krantz tells young female readers to "love and respect" themselves by getting enough sleep ("Betty always made sure she got enough sleep to keep refreshed and upbeat throughout the day"), keeping their homes tidy, spritzing their bedrooms with a delicate fragrance, eating plenty of greens and proteins, bathing in soap and water, taking care of their skin, and exercising regularly. Unfortunately, there's no indication that Betty did any of those things except keep her home tidy.

Sherrie Krantz's *How to Be a Betty* (2005) offers advice on everything from relationships to career advancement.

Krantz also tells her readers how they can dress like her subject. For instance, she notes that Betty "draws attention to her small waistline by wearing a more fitted look." She doesn't mention, however, that for prurient or romantic reasons, Betty occasionally lets the top of her dress fall down in public.

In a chapter titled, "How to Be a Betty at Work," Krantz advises young women to find a mentor and acknowledge their own strengths and weaknesses. Betty held numerous jobs at numerous levels of society, but it's not clear she did any of that. However, Krantz's advice is uniformly excellent.

After building a strong foundation, she advances into the subject her readers are probably most interested in—sex and dating. She discusses these topics thoroughly in her chapter titled, "How to Be a Betty in Love." Highlighting this sensible and well-written chapter is Krantz's suggestion that her readers shouldn't "fret and freak out if you get an 'I'm just not that into you' [message]."

"As silly and corny as it may sound," she writes, "you love yourself, and if that [other] person doesn't get it, well, your sense of self is solid as a rock." At this point Krantz might as well have been writing about Betty's on-and-off relationship with Bimbo. She also may have been referencing Betty's obviously solid self-confidence, which had inspired her to pursue Bimbo for several years without any significant reward.

Perhaps still thinking about Bimbo and his doggy inappropriateness, Krantz then asks her readers what would have happened if Betty had "settled for the wrong man? Where would her adventures be? Her sexy devilish spirit? Her delicious laugh? Her beautiful smile?" Good point, Krantz.

In Krantz's section on "Get-togethers and hangouts," she notes that those terms are "guy speak for 'booty call'" and advises her readers to "wait a bit, a few more dates, before you accept that kind of invitation." Betty does appear to have had sex on occasion, and Krantz's advice is probably right on the money.

In the final portion of her book, Krantz advises Betty's fans on the fine points of friendship and marriage. At this juncture, however, she probably should have reminded them that although Betty has appeared to engage in sex on various occasions over the years, she has never married or appeared to have had children. But maybe that's beside the point.

In any case, Krantz goes on to tell her readers quite accurately that "unleashing your own inner Boop" is "the most surefire and certain path to a life of sumptuous romance, endless adventure, and infinite Boop-oop-a-doops!"

The most recent Betty Boop guidebook is *Betty Boop's Guide to a Bold and Balanced Life: Fun, Fierce, Fabulous Advice Inspired by the Animated Icon,* released by Skyhorse Publishing in 2020. This book is not only well thought out and well written by Susan Wilking Horan and Kristi Ling Spencer, but was actually written "with Betty Boop," according to its cover and title page.

Horan and Spencer must have been glad to enlist Betty as a coauthor. "If there's one thing Betty knows, it's how to make a lasting impression," the three authors write in the book's introduction. "For more than ninety years, the glamorous international icon has sung, sashayed, and 'Boop-Oop-a-Dooped' past rules and conventions, unafraid to take risks or set trends, and proving time after time that she can do anything she sets her mind to."

In their thirty-seventh chapter, "Embrace Your Independence," Horan, Spencer, and Boop make an excellent case for Betty's current relevance to women's struggle for equality and independence. "While we have not lived through the changes of the last hundred years," they write, "our mothers, grandmothers, and great grandmothers have. And right next to them in the middle of the fight was our Betty. Her story is a reflection of our country's history, our personal history, and of women's history." Amen.

The most recent book to use Betty as a role model: *Betty Boop's Guide to a Bold and Balanced Life* (2020). Its authors are listed as "Susan Wilking Horan and Kristi Ling Spencer, with Betty Boop."

Horan, Spencer, and Boop also point out that not only has Betty held jobs as a nurse, seamstress, and schoolteacher, three traditional occupations for women, but that "Betty and the women of the time took the baton from their predecessors—women like Florence Nightingale and Susan B. Anthony—and ran confidently with it into the future." They go on to emphasize that "Betty was not only a part of [this development], but in many ways led the charge!"

The three authors note that soon after Amelia Earhart became the first woman to fly solo across the Atlantic, Betty ran for president. They also note that "just as Betty fought off unwanted advances by a lecherous circus ringmaster, women of the 1960s and 1970s began a long fight against sexual harassment in the workplace."

The trio goes on to urge women who are being sexually harassed to create a paper trail, get witnesses, and try to keep calm. (There's no evidence that Betty did any of these things except try to keep calm, but that was long before she started giving readers this excellent advice.)

Pointing out a very significant truth about Betty that the authors of the previous book ignored, they call her "the only female animated character in the world who has never been in a permanent relationship with a significant other. And she does just great!"

In their chapter on love, Horan, Spencer, and Boop touch gently on the fact that Betty's first lover was the dog-man Bimbo. Noting that "our hearts have limitless capacity for love, and how important it is to our vitality to welcome it in all of its manifestations," they go on to point out that "the love of our life might be . . . even a loving pet!" Later, they add that "the variety of love sources is endless."

Horan, Spencer, and Boop also zoom in on Betty as a style icon. Fashion designer Zac Posen was enlisted to write the book's foreword, which praises Betty's style. The book also points out that "Long before the famous image was cemented in our minds of Marilyn Monroe's dress blowing wildly upward from a subway vent, Betty introduced the iconic pose when her dress was "blowing wildly upward from the wind" in her 1932 cartoon "'Betty's Boop's Ups and Downs.'" (In that cartoon, actually, the earth loses its gravity because Saturn the Jew relieves it of its magnet, and Betty's skirt is blowing upward not because of the wind but because gravity no longer exists to hold down anyone's skirt.)

The authors also note that in 2017, Posen created two Betty Boop-inspired dress designs for his collection, and he and Betty went on to star in the animated short film *Betty Goes A-Posen*. Since then, Horan, Spencer, and Boop say, Betty has been busy with high-profile fashion collaborations including handbags, swimsuits, T-shirts, and other apparel featuring her iconic likeness. At the time, these items were being produced by Moschino, the streetwear band Supreme, and Yves Saint Laurent. Finally, Horan, Spencer, and Boop also remind their readers that in May 2019, Betty was celebrated by *Vogue* magazine as one of twenty-five "Camp Beauty Icons" along with stars such as Josephine Baker, Cher, and Grace Jones.

The book goes on to urge readers to imitate Betty by accentuating the positive, cultivating courage, demonstrating confidence, emphasizing humor, and taking care of one's health, all great goals. Betty was undoubtedly proud to be the coauthor of such a positive and helpful book, especially since it was based on her magnificent career so far.

Betty's legacy continues in all sorts of other cultural arenas. Consider Alison Moira Clarkson, a British woman who, because her face and attitude both resemble Betty's, dubbed herself "Betty Boop" before recording several pop-rap hits in the United Kingdom between 1989 and 1992. Although she remains a fan of Betty's, she was forced to drop the "Betty Boop" moniker prior to recording her songs to avoid trademark disputes. Now known as "Betty Boo," Clarkson wears short skirts, sings, and composes sassy music. Appropriately enough,

Cover for Betty Boo's 1992 album *Grrr! It's Betty Boo.*

her first album, "Boomania," was largely self-written and produced in her bedroom. Her latest single is "Get Me to the Weekend," released in 2022. Clarkson's career has been influential. When talent manager Chris Herbert was forming his all-female group, the Spice Girls, he told her that he was looking for five Betty Boops. (Clarkson's own backup dancers are known as the "Boosters.")

In a slightly inaccurate tribute to Betty's comic strip career, Clarkson performs onstage in front of numerous Marvel Comic–style graphics. And in an oblique reference to Betty's two on-screen runs for US president, Clarkson says she admired British prime minister Margaret Thatcher, although she didn't agree with Thatcher's politics, because she likes to see strong women in control. "I feel weak if I'm not in control," Clarkson said. "I always like to be in the driver's seat." Betty would certainly agree.

In 1996, Betty Boop, as opposed to Betty Boo, became the first cartoon character ever to be profiled on A&E's *Biography* series. Then, in 2002, *TV Guide* rated Betty number 17 in the list of the "50 Greatest Cartoon Characters of All Time."

In another indication of Betty Boop's powerful international appeal, a Serbian power pop girl band from Zrenjanin, Serbia, actually calls itself "Betty Boop." The band, which consists of five young women, won the New Star award at the Sunčane Skale festival in Herceg Novi in 2008. By 2010, it had released ten singles.

Betty herself starred annually from 2010 to 2012 at the Betty Boop Festival held during those years in Wisconsin Rapids, Wisconsin, the birthplace of her first animator, Grim Natwick. The festival exhibited the work of various cartoonists, including Natwick, and presented a live musical revue in which Broadway performer Tom Berklund led a cast that played music from the early Betty Boop era. In the evenings during the three festivals, Betty's fans gathered at a local tavern with Betty Boop collectibles expert Denis Hagopian.

Promotional poster for the 2010 Betty Boop festival in Wisconsin Rapids, Wisconsin, birthplace of Grim Natwick.

That annual festival also featured the rededication of a histori-cal marker honoring Natwick at the South Wood County Historical Museum, followed by a guided tour of the museum's Natwick and Betty Boop exhibit led by Stephen Worth, director of the Hollywood International Animation Society. These events were part of the annual three-day Grim Natwick Animated Film Festival that featured Betty's cartoons. The main portion of the festival ended each year with a large party known as the Betty Boop Bash, held on the festival's final evening.

In 2012, after polls indicated that 90 percent of American women aged eighteen to forty-nine recognized Betty, she starred in a Lancôme video. In this one-minute, fifty-two-second performance, Betty coun-sels model Daria Werbowy about using mascara. The video opens with Werbowy studying a script in a dressing room while struggling to say "Boop-Boop-a-Doop." Betty strolls in and tells Werbowy to "just say it with the eyes."

In the accompanying publicity, Lancôme pointed out that in Betty's cartoons, she sported five eyelashes on her top lid and four on the bot-tom one. Because the Boop-Werbowy video concentrated on Betty's eyes, she was provided with dozens of clusters of lashes for her appear-ance in it. Each cluster curled into a point.

In 2014, Russell Thomas, a barman at Alley Lounge in Los Angeles, expressed his admiration and affection for Betty by creating the Betty Boop cocktail. It's a mixture of two ounces of vodka or gin, one-half ounce of elderflower liqueur, three-quarters of an ounce of lime juice, five blackberries, one raspberry, and one-half ounce of simple syrup (or less, depending on the sweetness or tartness of the berries).

Thomas went on to suggest muddling in two to three blackberries, depending on their size, and one raspberry, and then adding ice. His

2012 print ad for Lancôme mascara featuring Betty.

next step is shaking the whole mixture, double straining it into a martini glass, and garnishing it with two blackberries on a spike.

Before COVID-19 sent many denizens of the entertainment world into hiding, several new Betty Boop productions were underway. Likely to be resumed after the pandemic is over, they include a Betty Boop musical, with music by David Foster and book by Oscar Williams and Sally Robinson. Meanwhile, Simon Cowell's Syco Entertainment, in partnership with Animal Logic, the company that animated *The Lego Movie*, have been working in Australia on a Betty Boop animated comedy fantasy movie that the company calls a "music-driven hybrid animated comedy" feature film.

"Betty is an icon, one of the biggest stars in the world, and I'm thrilled to be working with her," Cowell said. "Betty, I've worked with some serious divas, but I think you could be the biggest of them all!"

ACKNOWLEDGMENTS

MY THANKS to the world's greatest literary agent, Lee Sobel, for representing this book and several previous books of mine and for elevating my career to great heights; to the actress, activist, and playwright Kim Sykes, for giving me the idea of writing the biography of the great Betty Boop; and to my wife, Susan Harrigan, for supporting me in writing yet another book about an entertainer and for conscientiously editing several drafts of this one.

I also wish to extend my sincere thanks to my editor, Chris Chappell, who raised this manuscript from the dead with his skilled editorial suggestions and guidance; to his very helpful fellow editor John Cerullo; to Kim Sykes's husband, Tom Adcock, a prize-winning novelist who has been an inspiration to me for decades; to my hardworking archives agent, Sarah Funke Butler; to John Smyntek, a very accomplished journalist and editor who's been helping me for years; to Susan Schulman, the literary agent for Chicago Review Press, which published three of my previous books; to America's top music journalist and cultural critic, Greil Marcus; to my legal adviser Gregory Tanner; to my very supportive friend Bill Staiger; to my fellow Chicago Review Press author Tim Hanley; to my very supportive sister and brother,

ACKNOWLEDGMENTS

Wendy Benjaminson of Bloomberg News and retired US Ambassador Eric Benjaminson, and to my daughter Anne, her husband Greg Naarden, and my two grandchildren, Leo and Abby, for cheering me on as always.

I'd also like to thank my friends for encouraging and supporting me over several decades, including Roger Allen, David Anderson, Abid Aslam, Karlyn Barker, Steve Bergsman, Mark Boal, Jim Branson, John Brigham, Jennie Buckner, Barbara Butcher, Stephanie Campbell, Calhoun Cornwell, Irl Cramer, Alexandria Faiz, Barry Franklin, Larry Goldbetter, Janet Guyon, Barbara Hagerty, Duke Hagerty, Gervais Hagerty, Richard Hagerty, John Harrigan, Mary Harrigan, Lou Heldman, Len Hollie, Jean and David Horwatt, Ron Ishoy, Leroi Johnson, Ekim Kilic, Tim Kiska, Debbie Lovio, Jim Malley, Sheryl McCarthy, Ruth and Bernie Miller, Victoria Moran, Jill Morton, John Oppedahl, Tim Sheard, Susan Werbe, and Susan Whitall.

I'd also like to thank the other Boop enthusiasts who have written about Betty in their own books and essays on other subjects, all of whom are listed in the bibliography.

BIBLIOGRAPHY

Blogs and Websites

Animation Critique. Blog, May 16, 2008, at https://animationcritique .com/blog.

BettyBoop.com. https://www.bettyboop.com/

Betty Boop Fandom Wikipedia Website. https://bettyboop.fandom .com/wiki/Betty_Boop.

Popeye Cartoons (Formerly Popeye Animators). Blog, November 3, 2007.

Seymour Kneitel 1908–1964. Blog: The First Woman Animator. http:// seymourkneitel.blogspot.com/.

Books

Barrier, Michael. *Hollywood Cartoons: American Animation in Its Golden Age.* Oxford: Oxford University Press, 1999.

Beck, Jerry (ed.). *The 50 Greatest Cartoons as Selected by 1,000 Animation Professionals.* Nashville: Turner Publishing, 1994.

Brothers, Thomas. *Louis Armstrong: Master of Modernism.* New York: W.W. Norton & Co., 2014.

Byrd, Tweety. *Facts about Betty Boop from the Web.* Self-published, 2019.

Cabarga, Leslie. *The Fleischer Story.* New York: Da Capo Press, 1988.

Calloway, Cab, and Bryant Rollins. *Of Minnie the Moocher and Me.* New York: Thomas Y. Crowell Company, 1976.

Canemaker, John. *Felix: The Twisted Tale of the World's Most Famous Cat.* New York: Da Capo Press, 1986.

Cavalier, Stephen. *The World History of Animation.* Berkeley: University of California Press, 2011.

Cohen, Karl F. *Forbidden Animation: Censored Cartoons and Blacklisted Animators in America.* Jefferson, NC: McFarland and Company, 1997.

Culhane, Shamus. *Talking Animals and Other People: The Autobiography of One of Animation's Legendary Figures.* New York: St. Martin's Press, 1986.

———. *Animation from Script to Screen*, New York: St. Martin's Press, 1988.

Doherty, Thomas. *Pre-Code Hollywood: Sex, Immorality, and Insurrection in American Cinema, 1930–1934.* New York: Columbia University Press, 1999.

———. *Hollywood's Censor: Joseph I. Breen and the Production Code Administration.* New York: Columbia University Press, 2007.

Douglas, Ann. *Terrible Honesty: Mongrel Manhattan in the 1920s.* New York: Farrar, Straus and Giroux, 1996.

Fleischer, Max, and Bud Counihan. *The Definitive Betty Boop: The Classic Comic Strip Collection.* London: Titan Comics, 2015.

Fleischer, Richard, *Out of the Inkwell: Max Fleischer and the Animation Revolution.* Lexington: University Press of Kentucky, 2005.

Gilmore, Donald H. *Sex in Comics: A History of the Eight Pagers.* Volume 1. Austin, TX: Greenleaf Classics, 1971.

Goldmark, Daniel. *Tunes for 'Toons: Music and the Hollywood Cartoon.* Berkeley: University of California Press, 2005.

Grippo, Robert M., and Christopher Hoskins. *Macy's Thanksgiving Day Parade*. Mount Pleasant, SC: Arcadia Publishing, 2004.

Hackney, Rick. *Starring Betty Boop*. Larkspur, CA: Determined Productions Inc., 1984.

Halberstam, David. *The Coldest Winter: America and the Korean War*. New York: Hachette Books, 2008.

Hanley, Tim. *Wonder Woman Unbound: The Curious History of the World's Most Famous Heroine*. Chicago: Chicago Review Press, 2014.

———. *Investigating Lois Lane: The Turbulent History of the Daily Planet's Ace Reporter*. Chicago: Chicago Review Press, 2016.

———. *The Many Lives of Catwoman: The Felonious History of a Feline Fatale*. Chicago: Chicago Review Press, 2017.

Horan, Susan Wilking, and Kristi Ling Spencer, with Betty Boop. *Betty Boop's Guide to a Bold and Balanced Life: Fun, Fierce, Fabulous Advice Inspired by the Animated Icon*. New York: Skyhorse Publishing, 2020.

Horn, Maurice. *Sex in the Comics*. New York: Chelsea House Publishers, 1985.

Huggins, Nathan Irvin. *Harlem Renaissance*. Cambridge, MA: Harvard University Press, 1971.

Kanfer, Stefan. *Serious Business: The Art and Commerce of Animation in America from Betty Boop to "Toy Story."* New York: Da Capo Press, 1997.

Krantz, Sherrie. *How to Be a Betty: The Ultimate Guide to Unleashing Your Inner Boop!* New York: Ballantine Books, 2020.

Lawson, Tim, and Alisa Persons. *The Magic Behind the Voices: A Who's Who of Cartoon Voice Actors*. Jackson: University Press of Mississippi, 2004.

BIBLIOGRAPHY

Lehman, Christopher P. *The Colored Cartoon: Black Representation in American Animated Short Films, 1907–1954*. Amherst: University of Massachusetts Press, 2007.

Lenberg, Jeff. *Who's Who in Animated Cartoons*. New York: Applause Theatre & Cinema Books, 2006.

Lepore, Jill. *The Secret History of Wonder Woman*. New York: Vintage Books, 2015.

Maltin, Leonard. *Of Mice and Magic: A History of American Animated Cartoons*. New York: Penguin, 1987.

McGowan, David. *Animated Personalities*. Austin: University of Texas Press, 2019.

Michaelis, David. *Schultz and Peanuts: A Biography*. New York: Harper Perennial, 2008.

Mitenbuler, Reid. *The Artists and Rivalries That Inspired the Golden Age of Animation*. New York: Atlantic Monthly Press, 2020.

Nicholson, Hope. *The Spectacular Sisterhood of Superwomen*. Philadelphia: Quirk Books, 2017.

Norton, Jack. *Dirty Little Comics: A Pictorial History of Tijuana Bibles and Underground Adult Comics of the 1920s–1950s*. N.P.: J&K Norton Family Publishing, 2020.

Pointer, Ray. *The Art and Inventions of Max Fleischer, American Animation Pioneer*. Jefferson, NC: MacFarland and Company, 2017.

Quagmire, Joshua. *Betty Boop's Big Break*. Chicago: First Publishing Inc., 1990.

Rose Marie. *Hold the Roses, The Autobiography of Rose Marie*. Lexington: University Press of Kentucky, 2002.

Shipton, Alyn. *Hi-De-Ho: The Life of Cab Calloway*. Oxford: Oxford University Press, 2010.

Smoodin, Eric. *Animating Culture: Hollywood Cartoons from the Sound Era*. New Brunswick, NJ: Rutgers University Press, 1993.

Solomon, Charles. *Enchanted Drawings: The History of Animation*. New York: Wings Books, 2004.

Sullivan, Robert (ed.). *America's Parade: A Celebration of Macy's Thanksgiving Day Parade*. New York: Time Home Entertainment, 2001.

Taylor, James D. Jr. *Helen Kane and Betty Boop: On Stage and on Trial*. New York: Algora Publishing, 2017.

———. *The Voice of Betty Boop, Mae Questel*. New York: Algora Publishing, 2020.

Tye, Larry. *Superman: The High-Flying History of America's Most Enduring Hero*. New York: Random House, 2012.

Viera, Mark. *Forbidden Hollywood: The Pre-Code Era (1930–1934), When Sin Ruled the Movies*. New York: Running Press Adult, 2019.

Weldon, Glen. *The Caped Crusade: Batman and the Rise of Nerd Culture*. New York: Simon & Schuster, 2016.

———. *Superman: The Unauthorized Biography*. Hoboken, NJ: Wiley, 2013.

West, Wallace. *Betty Boop in Snow-White*. Atlanta, GA: Whitman Publishing Company, 1934.

Young, Dean, and Rick Marschall. *Blondie and Dagwood's America*. New York: Harper & Row, 1981.

Animated Cartoons and Non-animated Movies

As discussed in book (in order of and followed by release dates)

The Cabinet of Dr. Caligari, March 19, 1920

"Karnival Kid," May 23, 1929

Un Chien Andalou, June 6, 1929

"Hot Dog," March 29, 1930

"Dizzy Dishes," August 9, 1930

"Barnacle Bill the Sailor," August 25, 1930

"Mysterious Mose," December 29, 1930

"The Bum Bandit," April 6, 1931

"Silly Scandals," May 23, 1931

"Bimbo's Initiation," July 27, 1931

"Betty Co-Ed," August 1, 1931

"Bimbo's Express," August 22, 1931

"Minding the Baby," September 28, 1931

"Girls about Town," November 7, 1931

"Mask-A-Raid," November 9, 1931

"Dizzy Red Riding Hood," December 12, 1931

"Any Rags," January 5, 1932

"Boop-Oop-A-Doop," January 16, 1932

"Minnie the Moocher," March 3, 1932

"Chess Nuts," April 18, 1932

"A-Hunting We Will Go," May 3, 1932

"Let Me Call You Sweetheart," May 20, 1932

"Admission Free," June 12, 1932

"Red-Headed Woman," June 25, 1932

"Stopping the Show," August 12, 1932

"Betty Boop's Bamboo Isle," September 23, 1932

"Betty Boop's Ups and Downs," October 14, 1932

"Betty Boop for President," November 4, 1932

"I'll Be Glad When You're Dead You Rascal You," November 25, 1932

"Betty Boop Meets Dracula," 1933

"Betty Boop's Crazy Inventions," January 27, 1933

"Is My Palm Read," February 17, 1933

"Snow-White," March 3, 1933

"Betty Boop's Penthouse," March 10, 1933

"Three Little Pigs," May 21, 1933

"Betty Boop's Big Boss," June 2, 1933

"Popeye the Sailor," July 14, 1933

"The Old Man of the Mountain," August 4, 1933

"I Heard," September 1, 1933

"She Wronged Him Right," January 5, 1934

"Sock-a-Bye Baby," January 19, 1934

"Red Hot Mamma," February 2, 1934

"Ha! Ha! Ha!" March 2, 1934

"Betty in Blunderland," April 6, 1934

"Betty Boop's Rise to Fame," May 18, 1934

"Betty Boop's Trial," June 15, 1934

"Betty Boop's Lifeguard," July 13, 1934

"Poor Cinderella," August 3, 1934

"There's Something about a Soldier," August 17, 1934

"Betty Boop's Little Pal," September 21, 1934

"Betty Boop's Prize Show," October 19, 1934

"No, No, a Thousand Times No," May 24, 1935

"A Language All My Own," July 19, 1935

"Betty Boop and Grampy," August 16, 1935

"You Gotta Be a Football Hero," August 31, 1935

"Making Stars," October 18, 1935

"Betty Boop with Henry, The Funniest Living American," November 22, 1935

"Little Nobody," December 18, 1935

"A Song a Day!" May 22, 1936

"Grampy's Indoor Outing," October 16, 1936

"Be Human," November 20, 1936

Snow White and the Seven Dwarfs, February 4, 1937

"Pudgy Takes a Bow-Wow, April 9, 1937

"The Impractical Joker," June 18, 1937

"Zula Hula," December 24, 1937

"Pudgy the Watchman," August 12, 1938

"Sally Swing," October 14, 1938

"The Scared Crows," June 9, 1939

"Rhythm on the Reservation," July 7, 1939

"Marry-Go-Round," December 31, 1943

"Betty Boop for President," November 4, 1932 and November 21, 1980

"The Romance of Betty Boop," March 20, 1985

Who Framed Roger Rabbit, June 22, 1988

Televised Documentaries about Betty

Betty Boop: Boop Oop A Doop, hosted by Steve Allen, 1985

Betty Boop: The Queen of Cartoons, A&E Biography Series, A&E Television Network, 1995

Cartoon Crazys Banned and Censored, Sound-Track Enhancements & Audio Galaxy Inc., 2000

Wait for Your Laugh documentary, 2018

Comic Strips (Newspaper)

Betty Boop, black-and-white comic strips appearing daily in more than 100 American newspapers from July 15, 1934, through March 18, 1935, King Features Inc.

Betty Boop, full-page full-colored comic strips appearing on Sundays in many US newspapers from November 15, 1934, through August 21, 1937, King Features Inc.

Helen Kane, full-page full-colored colored comic strips appearing on Sundays in the *New York Mirror* from August 5, 1934, through October 12, 1934, King Features Inc.

Adult Comic Strips

"Betty Steps Out," 1935, Anonymous

"Betty Boop in Flesh," 1935, Anonymous

"Betty Boop in Hot Pants," 1935, Anonymous

"Improvising," 1935, Anonymous

Magazine and Anthology Articles

Austen, Jake, "Hidey Hidey Hidey Ho . . . Boop-Boop-A-Doop!" in *The Cartoon Music Book*, eds. Goldmark, Daniel, and Yuval Taylor, 61–66. Chicago: A Capella, 2002.

Dobbs, G. Michael. "Happy Birthday Betty!" *Animato! The Animation Fan's Magazine*, Fall, 1985.

Franklin, Mortimer, "The Love Life of Betty Boop," *Screenland Magazine*, January 1933.

Hurd, Jud, "Betty Boop and Felix Meet the Walker Brothers," *Cartoonist Profiles*, December 1984.

Rose Marie, "'*Dick Van Dyke*' Star Rose Marie: 'What Happened When I Publicly Shamed My Harasser,'" *Hollywood Reporter*, December 7, 2017.

Newspaper Articles and Dates of Publication

Arizona Republic, "Betty Boop's Creator, 'Grim' Natwick, Dies," October 9, 1990.

Bellingham Herald, "Now Premiering: The Betty Boop Porcelain Collector Doll," February 4, 1996.

Calgary Herald, "Boop-Oop-A-Doop," May 26, 1985.

Daily Tribune (Wisconsin Rapids, Wisconsin), "Animation by Grim Natwick," July 7, 1984; "100 Years Old: Grim Natwick, the Local Man Who Created Betty Boop, Turns 100," August 16, 1990; "Local Festival a Reminder to Dream Big," August 7, 2010; and "Betty Boop Collection Grows Through the Years," July 30, 2011.

The Des Moines Register, "Boopaholic Has Amassed Huge Collection in a Short Time," October 27, 2001.

The Detroit News, "Betty Boop Stamps Cause Sensation!! Post Office Finally Honors Flapper," June 5, 2021.

Intelligencer Journal/Lancaster New Era, Lancaster, PA, "Balloons Are Thanksgiving Crowd-Pleasers," February 26, 1993, and "Betty Boop: 30s Flirty Spit-Curled Cartoon Sparks Boopiana," November 21, 2012.

Los Angeles Times, "Honoring Two Enduring Styles of Celluloid," March 3, 1990, and "Shop Has Specialty Gifts, Collectibles, Betty Boop Items," February 7, 1991.

Marshfield (Wisconsin) *News-Herald*, "Life Magazine Parades Out Book," November 18, 2001.

Miami Herald, "Collectors Still Like Cartoon Betty Boop," June 25, 1995.

New York Daily News, "Macy's Thanksgiving Day Parade" November 27, 1985; "Gobbling Up Turkey Day Treats," November 29, 1985;

"Weather or Not, the Big Macy's Parade Reigns," November 22, 1987; "Miracle on 77th Street," November 28, 1991; "Here Come the Parades! TV Trots out its Traditional Turkey Day Trimmings," November 26, 1992; "He Reigns on Parade: Confessions of Confirmed Balloon-atic," May 12, 1995; "Betty Boop is Back in the Burg: The Daring Oop-a-Doop Darling of the Depression Has a Forum Fortnight Fling," November 22, 1995; "Parade Line-Up" and "It's Been a Rocky Road, But Bullwinkle's Back," November 7, 1996.

Rutland (VT) Daily Herald, "Betty Boop Checks," October 11, 1998.

Sacramento Bee, "Betty Boop's Bumps," July 4, 1981.

The Saint Joseph (MI) News Press, "Woman Who Played Betty Boop Now Ordained Minister," June 27, 1971.

Sentinel (Carlisle, PA), "Betty Boop Remains Popular After 68 Years," July 5, 1998.

South Bend (IN) Tribune, "Girl Gets Job of Animating Film Cartoons," October 22, 1934, and "Newlywed Inherits Betty Boop Memorabilia Cache," April 30, 2004.

South Idaho Press (Burley, Idaho), "Boop Stamps Drive Collectors Wild!" July 31, 2000.

The Star Press (Muncie, Indiana), "Boop-Oop-A-Doop: Muncie Woman Likes to Start and End Her Day with a Boop Character," November 10, 2006.

Tampa Bay Times (St. Petersburg, Florida), "Parimutuels: Tampa Dog Track," August 23, 2001.

Tensas Gazette (Saint Joseph, Louisiana), "1999 All-America Rose Winners Selection Available," January 20, 1999.

The Times and Democrat (Orangeburg, SC), "Betty Boop Returns—on Big Shirts," March 23, 1986.

INDEX

Page references for figures are italicized.